Basenji

◇

By Juliette Cunliffe

Contents

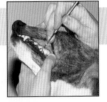

KENNEL CLUB BOOKS: BASENJI
ISBN: 1-59378-308-6

Copyright © 2005 • Kennel Club Books, LLC
308 Main Street, Allenhurst, NJ 07711 USA
Cover Design Patented: US 6,435,559 B2 • Printed in South Korea

Photography by Cheryl A. Ertelt & Carol Ann Johnson
with additional photographs by

Paulette Braun, T.J. Calhoun, Alan and Sandy Carey, Carolina Biological Supply, Isabelle Français, A. Jemolo, Bill Jonas, Dr. Dennis Kunkel, Tam C. Nguyen, Phototake, Jean Claude Revy, Alice Roche, Kent Standerford, Karen Taylor and Alice van Kempen.

Illustrations by Patricia Peters.

The publisher wishes to thank all of the owners of the dogs featured in this book including Jan Caton, Janette Hahn, Suzanne LaCroix and Carol Ann Worsham.

Detail of an Egyptian papyrus, circa 900 BC, showing the night voyage of the sun god in his boat. The boat is being pulled by four jackals, which bear a resemblance to today's Basenji and some of the sighthound breeds.

HISTORY OF THE

BASENJI

The Basenji is a very special dog, used in Africa as an all-around hunter and typifying neither a classic sighthound nor scenthound, as it hunts by both scent and sight. It appears to have developed from a diversity of canid types and indeed is probably most closely related to the pariah family. Over the years, the breed has also been described as both a terrier and as one of the spitz breeds, so to obtain a clearer picture of the Basenji we will peruse the pages of history.

Today's Basenji is the descendant of a dog well known to the pharaohs of Egypt, for rock carvings dating back about 5,000 years tell us of the breed's history in that land. There is no doubt that remarkably similar dogs were in Upper Egypt at one time, and probably also in Lower Egypt. The Khufu dogs are the first domestic dogs to have been known in ancient Egypt, found on tombs in the period of King Khufu (also known as Cheops), who reigned from 2,638 until 2,613 BC. Although they have been described as being of spitz type, they are more likely to have resembled the dingo/pariah type,

A painted wooden statue from the early Ptolemaic period, circa 300 BC, of the jackal-headed Anubis, god of death.

There were even accounts of individual dogs, so we know that they were well thought of by both the pharaohs themselves and by court officials. There is a remarkable account of a Basenji-type dog by the name of Abuwtiyuw, who was buried in fine linen. The following inscription was found on an ancient Egyptian tomb of about 2,650 BC and is well deserving of quotation to set the scene:

"The dog which was the guard of His Majesty,
Abuwtiyuw is his name.
His Majesty ordered that he be buried ceremonially,
That he be given a coffin from the Royal treasury,
Fine linen in great quantity, and incense.
His Majesty also gave perfumed ointment, and ordered that a tomb
Be built for him by gangs of masons.
His Majesty did this for him in order that the dog
Might be honored before the great god, Anubis."

It is likely that many dogs similar to the Basenji we know today were entombed with great honors, especially those belonging to the royal household. It should, however, be recognized that Egyptian dogs more akin to the Greyhound were also honored in this way.

but certainly show strong Basenji characteristics. It is evident that some, at least, were kept as house dogs, for they were shown on the chairs of their masters and were named "thesam," which means "hound" or "ordinary dog."

With the fall of the Egyptian pharaohs and as trading routes opened up, various tribes throughout the Congo adopted the dogs that had been so favored in Egypt. Merchants must have traveled with their dogs, and so the breed spread farther into Africa. In Central Africa, the Basenji was reputed to be very attached to its masters, and the affection was reciprocated. They were put to several different kinds of tasks; in particular, hunting and destroying the long-toothed reed rat that was a great threat to the natives' homesteads and to their livestock. The Basenji also was used by native hunters as a beater of game and for hunting antelope. As a sporting dog, the Basenji is both fast and agile, and a remarkably good jumper. In Africa, it can jump sufficiently high to see over the tall elephant grass, for which reason it is sometimes known as the *M'bwa m'kubwa M'mwa mamwitu*, which can be roughly translated as "jumping-up-and-down-dog."

When working as a beating dog, a so-called "king" dog was selected to lead the beaters. As the Basenji did not use its voice, around its neck was tied a dried gourd, filled with pebbles, which would make noise.

In Central Africa, the Basenji found itself with many close relatives, among which were the Niam Niam and the Manbouton. It also found itself with a variety of names—Belgian Congo Dog, Congo Bush Dog, Congo Hunting Terrier, Lagos Bush Dog and Congo Terrier were all commonly used for this breed.

DESCRIPTION OF THE CONGO TERRIER

Writing in 1906, Robert Leighton gave a description of the Congo Terrier and incorporated a picture of "Bosc," who was kept in the Zoological Gardens in Paris. He wrote of the Congo Terrier as being one of the most authentic of African breeds, a symmetrical, lightly built dog.

CANIS LUPUS

"Grandma, what big teeth you have!" The gray wolf, a familiar figure in fairy tales and legends, has had its reputation tarnished and its population pummeled over the centuries. Yet it is the descendants of this much-feared creature to which we open our homes and hearts. Our beloved dog, *Canis domesticus*, derives directly from the gray wolf, a highly social canine that lives in elaborately structured packs. In the wild, the gray wolf can range from 60 to 175 pounds, standing between 25 and 40 inches in height.

Sitting in the celebrated Anubis fashion, the Basenji is a thoroughbred aristocrat with a long and proud history.

FACING PAGE: In the burial vault of Pashedu, about 1,150 BC, Anubis jackals, on royal pedestals, are guarding access to the vault. Notice their resemblance to the Basenji.

Leighton may have meant a scissor bite. The short tail was usually curved over the back and was somewhat bushy.

Interestingly, the writer comments on a ridge of longer hair along the spine, even though the rest of the coat was short. This surely leads one to make some connection with the Rhodesian Ridgeback, also an African breed. The color was red or mouse-gray, with large white patches. Leighton comments further that Sir Harry Johnston had noticed that "these dogs were much used for terrier work in the territory north of the Zambesi. In a degenerate state they become pariah dogs, and as such may often be seen prowling about the Congo villages."

A "BARKLESS" DOG?
Although the Basenji as a breed is unique, there have been rather far-fetched stories about the

Though he described a rather long head, large upstanding ears and intelligent, dark eyes, the size varied enormously, from 12 to 24 inches tall. This is a much wider range in height than in today's Basenji; thus, the early dogs were seen both much shorter and much taller than the modern breed. Teeth were well developed "but mostly over-shot," though, of course, by this

YODELING IN THE CONGO
Known as "the barkless dog," the Basenji is, in fact, capable of barking, but its vocal cords are not really shaped for barking. The reason the Basenji makes sounds different from those of other dogs is because the larynx is not located in the same place as it is in others. The result is a wide variety of delightful vocalizations, including yodels, chortles, mumbles and others that you just have to hear to understand!

A PRIZED POSSESSION

Among its many practical functions in Africa, the Basenji was used to hunt the reed rat, a vicious long-toothed animal weighing 12–20 pounds. The Basenji's silent manner of working proved a great asset. Basenjis also have wonderful noses and can scent at a distance of 80 yards.

The value placed on Basenjis by African natives was high indeed, for they not only hunted antelope and a large species of reed rat but they also were capable of driving larger game. Their worth was more than 20 times the value of a spear.

breed's being absolutely mute and unable to bark. It is true enough that the Basenji is a quiet dog and normally does not bark, but with the exception of a terrier's yap and a hound's bay, it is, when excited, capable of all other canine sounds and has a few interesting sounds all his own. The Basenji is not alone in this, as some other Equatorial dogs utter their sounds in a gentle murmur that can increase to a chortle, which rather resembles a yodeling sound. The Basenji uses this sound to express pleasure. It is interesting to note that the wolf, too, is capable of barking, though it seldom does so.

THE BASENJI GOES TO BRITAIN

Two Basenjis, entered as Lagos Bush Dogs, were exhibited at the Crufts Dog Show in the 1890s. These dogs were red and white, with white on their necks, "rather dingo-headed, and decidedly breedy-looking," and it was noted they could not bark properly. Sadly, both died of distemper shortly after the show.

In the 1920s, Lady Helen Nutting owned six Basenjis in the Sudan; these she kept in Khartoum before bringing them to England. Unfortunately, all of them died due to the effects of the distemper inoculation, something that was then only in an experimental stage. Despite this dreadful experience, she retained her interest in the breed for many years to come.

In the 1930s, Mrs. Olivia Burn, who lived near Canterbury, brought home her Basenjis from Central Africa, and took advice from the noted canine author Mr. A. Croxton Smith as to how best she could obtain publicity for them. He suggested that she show them at Crufts the following year, so they were exhibited at Islington's Royal Agricultural Hall in 1937. Upon meeting the dogs, Croxton Smith thought the breed was well worth encouraging, for they were of a convenient size and yet looked sporting and intelligent.

Mrs. Burn had first seen the dogs when she was visiting her husband, who was holding an appointment in the Kwango district up the Kwillo River, a tributary of the Congo. Mrs. Burn was the breeder of the well-known Blean Wirehaired Fox Terriers, and she was immediately attracted to the hunting dogs she saw living with the Africans. In inquiring what the breed was called, the nearest name she could get was "Basenji," which translates to "bush thing," or "little thing of the bush." The dogs she chose came from those bred by tribal chiefs, and their long journey back to England involved river steamer, train and plane. Mrs. Burn subsequently imported a number of other Basenjis and had them sent by plane, via Antwerp.

As the Crufts show of 1937 approached, Croxton Smith wrote a paragraph about these remarkable dogs that made only a crooning noise, and his article captured the imagination of the press. Reporters and photographers visited Mrs. Burn and her dogs, and the papers were full of them. Considered eccentricities, they were "dogs-with-a-difference," members of a breed that "crooned and washed itself like a cat." When Crufts opened, there was a long line of people in Upper Islington Street, reputedly made up of people all waiting to see the "barkless dogs." The breed had certainly hit the headlines!

THE BASENJI ENTERS THE US

The year 1937 marks the official beginning of the Basenji in the United States, as this was the year in which Mrs. Olivia Burn exported three Basenjis to Mr. and Mrs. Byron Rogers of New York. This trio included the male Bakuma of Blean and two bitches that died a year after importation. Bakuma mysteriously disappeared. The next imports to the US came to Dr. A.R.B. Richmond from Toronto in 1939, these from English breeder Veronica Tudor-Williams and her Congo kennel. This pair died of distemper. In 1940, a quartet arrived to Dr. Richmond: these were males Kwillo and Koodoo of the Congo, and females Kikuyu and Kiteve of the Congo. Kwillo became a Canadian Champion in 1942, the first Basenji champion in any country.

It was in 1941 that Alexander and Mary Phemister of Massachusetts acquired a bitch

FAMOUS OWNERS

Several famous people have owned Basenjis over the years. Among them have been Queen Juliana of the Netherlands and members of the Romanian royal family.

named Congo, a stowaway on a coffee boat from Africa. Congo was bred to Koodoo of the Congo, purchased by the Phemisters from Dr. Richmond. They produced Phemister's Barrie, who became the first obedience-titled Basenji. A lost Basenji was purchased by the Phemisters, and he was named Phemister's Bois. Photographs reveal that Bois was actually Bakuma of Blean, who had disappeared a few years prior. He became an important sire for the breed, though he wasn't a champion.

The arrival of the Basenji to the US received more media attention than most other dog importations. An issue of *Life* magazine from 1941 featured a photo of a Basenji in a cargo crate, coming from Africa with two gorillas. The caption described the breed as "mute but fearless," as the photo depicted the Basenji chasing the gorilla around the large container. There actually were four Basenjis that were shipped in this gorilla carrier, among them Kasenyi and Kindu, the first Basenjis to be shown at the Westminster Kennel Club show ("for exhibition only") in 1942. They were obtained by Mrs. Tress Taaffee of California the following year and became the foundation of her kennel.

Interest in the breed

> **DOGS FIRST**
>
> Travelers to Africa in the 1930s were somewhat surprised at the attitude of the natives to their Basenjis, when compared with that shown toward their children. When a truck approached, they were seen to run and pick up their dogs while their toddlers, also standing in the road, were ignored!

increased and the Basenji Club of America (BCOA) was formed in 1942, with Mr. Phemister as the club's first president. The club accepted the breed standard that had been drawn up by the Basenji Club of Great Britain. The American Kennel Club (AKC) accepted the standard on November 9, 1943, and the Basenji became eligible for registration. There was a total of about 35 Basenjis registered; registrations climbed up to 59 within a few short months. At this point, the breed was recognized for registration purposes, but not for showing in individual Basenji classes. Because of a new AKC rule in 1943, all newly recognized breeds could only be shown in Miscellaneous Classes.

The first champion Basenji was sired by Phemister's Bois out of Zinnia of the Congo: Ch. Phemister's Melengo earned the title in 1945. His dam then earned the title in 1946. A Basenji named Ch. Kingolo earned the champion title in 1949; he was the son of Kindu and Kasenyi, two of the Basenjis that arrived with the gorillas. The Basenji Club of America held its first specialty show in 1950, and the famous dog authority Alva Rosenberg served as judge. Ch. Rhosenji Beau, owned by George Gilky, was selected as Best of Breed.

Another important first was won by Am./Can. Ch. Dainty Dancer of Glenairley in 1958. She was the first Basenji to win a Best in Show in the US. The year prior, when she was nine months of age, she won the first Canadian Best in Show. She was handled by Bob Hastings and won a total of seven Bests in Show.

Basenjis in North America by 1960 were essentially red and white, which remains the most popular color today. Miss Tudor-Williams and two other fanciers visited southern Sudan in 1959 and reported on the condition and coloration of the African dogs. They found over half the dogs to be chestnut with white and one-quarter to be tricolor (black, white and tan), as well as one black and white dog and one tiger-striped brindle. Most of the dogs that they saw were Basenji-like village dogs, though not many true breed examples. Two

The Basenji possesses a regal look and an air of mystery befitting its mythological past.

dogs were exported to England, Fula of the Congo and Tiger of the Congo, the former having done much for the breed worldwide to improve type and temperament and the latter (later named M'Binza of Laughing Brook) was the first brindle export. Miss Tudor-Williams, now regarded as one of the Basenji's saviors, summed up the breed's passage to the West by stating that "practically every Basenji in the world consists of: Bongo, Bereke, Bokoto, Bashele and Bungwa of Blean, Amatangazig, Wau and Fula of the Congo and Kindu and

DIVINING DOGS

In the Congo, if people fell ill repeatedly, this was believed to have been caused by black magic. Wooden instruments representing dogs (called divining dogs) were presented with the names of possible sorcerers upon them. The knob attached to the wooden dog's back was then briskly rubbed up and down, and the name at which it became stuck was believed to be the sorcerer responsible.

Kasenyi through their son, Ch. Kingolo." Two other Basenjis, added to the list by author Susan Coe, are Kiki of Cryon, a black and white import from Africa, and Phemister's Bois, both of which can be found on Basenji pedigrees to this day. In 1980 a publication called *Years of the American Basenji* was released. It is an important record of American breed history that has continued to this day, currently running five looseleaf volumes, with over 4,000 American titled Basenjis shown on its pages—all descendants of the original twelve.

A new chapter in Basenji history opened up in 1987, when American breeders Jon Curby and Michael Work went on a Basenji-seeking excursion to Africa. They reported that of the nearly 300 dogs they observed, about half of them were brindle. This proved to be quite a revelation to the Basenji community worldwide. The following year, Curby along with two other fanciers, Damara Bolte and Stan Carter, traveled to Zaire and brought back 14 Basenjis, including a dam in whelp. The brindle imports caused quite a stir in AKC circles. What was fascinating to breed historians was the fact that there seemed to be little difference between the dogs imported into the US in the 1930s and 1940s and the more recent imports, except that the dogs from the 1980s seemed less feral and more approachable than the earlier dogs.

The allure of lure coursing! Basenjis excel in this exciting sporting event because of their keen sight and great speed.

Breeders were keen to include these new imports into existing American bloodlines, though the AKC long had forbidden registration of African stock. The Basenji Club of America voted to accept the new imports as well as to revise the breed standard to include the brindle coloration. By 1990, the AKC agreed to accept the revision to the standard and two-thirds of the imported dogs (13 of the total 21 dogs imported). These dogs were given the Avongara prefix and were used in breeding programs. Since the early 1990s, there have been many champions with the Avongara dogs in their pedigrees.

The Basenji Club of America is a member of the AKC and has over 500 members, not only in the US but in other countries too. There are 21 regional clubs affiliated with the BCOA. Apart from sanctioned conformation matches, the club also holds obedience and lure-coursing trials. That Basenjis compete in obedience, agility and field events speaks well for this intelligent trainable dog. In the early days, you could hardly drag a Basenji into the obedience ring; nowadays, there are Basenjis with Utility Dog titles!

Lure coursing, of course, has its allure for Basenjis! Lyle Gillette and other sighthound fanciers from California

developed lure coursing as a performance event in the early 1970s. Gillette and her band had hunted jackrabbits in open field, but recognized that a safer, more controlled sport would be beneficial. Lure coursing uses pullies to simulate the running and turning actions of live prey. Together they formed the American Sighthound Field Association (ASFA) in 1972. Nearly two decades later, in 1991, the AKC approved lure coursing regulations and also sanctioned the sport.

Today Basenjis participate both in ASFA and AKC lure-coursing events, and it is indeed a spectacular sight to watch dogs using every muscle in their chase of an evasive lure that is, in reality, nothing more than a white trash bag attached to a cable system. The limitless Basenji may take part in sanctioned AKC conformation, obedience, agility, lure-coursing and tracking tests.

Evidence of the tractable personality of today's Basenji, a Basenji participates in an obedience class with other breeds.

BASENJI

Naturally, it should be appreciated that the Basenji is certainly not the breed for everyone. A Basenji owner needs both patience and flexibility to understand this unusual breed, but for such people the Basenji will give many years of devoted companionship and pleasure. An affectionate pet, the Basenji, with his sleek and highly attractive appearance, makes a wonderful companion and should always be treated as such. Indeed, with a Basenji around the house, which is the place he prefers, it is difficult to be lonely!

The Basenji is an expressive dog described in the 1930s as "half an angel, half a cat." Some say that a Basenji is like a cat trapped inside the body of a dog. Basenjis are regal dogs, but are subject to sudden bouts of absolute canine joy and can go from a statuesque pose into berserk play-mode in just a matter of seconds.

This is a particularly clean breed, one that washes itself thoroughly in the manner of a cat and likes to be involved in anything that involves cleaning. Washing clothes apparently holds endless fascination for them! After a walk in the rain, Basenjis enjoy drying each other off. Another cat-like trait is the way that Basenjis use their front paws in a similar fashion.

Basenjis are capable of running for miles without tiring, for they are very fit and athletic dogs. They are reputed, though, to have very little

COMFORTS OF HOME

Although Basenjis frequently enjoy chewing furniture, they do love their comforts and seem to feel it their prerogative to recline on any piece of furniture.

road sense, so they must be carefully and sensibly controlled (i.e., *on leash!*) when near traffic (not too many busy intersections in the Congo!).

It should be remembered that the Basenji is a hunter by nature, and as a result many need plenty of opportunity for activity to keep them happily occupied and out of trouble. Some need long full-out runs to use up their energy, although others seem to be content with good long walks. Again, safety is important. Any off-lead exercise must be in safely enclosed areas to prevent your Basenji from going off running, "hunting" something that strikes his interest.

PERSONALITY

The American Kennel Club breed standard describes the Basenji as intelligent and independent, but affectionate and alert. It also mentions that the breed can be aloof with strangers, and this is a serious consideration when deciding on whether or not a Basenji is the most suitable dog to fit your family's lifestyle.

An inquisitive breed that likes to participate in every possible activity, the Basenji seems to enjoy teasing his owners. However, he does not like to be foolishly teased back, for he is quite dignified about his curiosity and basically has a serious nature. Basenjis tend to be rather dominant dogs and have a tendency to think deeply before

ANYONE FOR A SWIM?
Although there are exceptions, most Basenjis do not like water and would be highly reluctant to go for a swim. Perhaps because they are so fastidious about their own appearance, they will do their best to avoid water. A walk in the rain is also generally frowned upon! However, there are reports of some with close African ancestry enjoying a cooling soak during the hottest parts of the day.

deciding to obey orders.

An owner must discipline a Basenji justly if he expects to win the dog's respect. Basenjis should not be allowed to get away with mischief, for most owners will agree that the Basenji in general can be described as a "naughty" breed. It is essential, though, that the dog knows exactly why he is being reprimanded. A young Basenji will almost undoubtedly try things out on his owners, just as a child might. This can be a challenge to an owner, but discipline must be given and parameters established; this aspect of a Basenji's upbringing and care should never be overlooked.

Another feature of a Basenji's

GOOD CHEWERS

Many Basenjis are chewers. They enjoy chewing anything available, and this includes not only socks and shoes but also chairs, sofas, rocks, fences and trees. For this reason, when they go out many owners leave their dogs in sizeable crates with something safe to chew upon. Such a precaution can avoid much distress to the dog's digestive system as well as the owner's belongings.

personality is that he has a long memory. This will enable him to remember not only his training guidelines but also people and places; he will also remember what he has liked and disliked previously. If treated well, he is almost certain to feel that his own family can do no wrong in his eyes, but it is his owner's duty to teach him that the world outside his own home can also be a place of happiness. The Basenji will need to be taken outside the home environment to socialize and establish his confidence.

"BARKLESS," BUT NOT MUTE
Basenjis make their own special noises, which sometimes can sound like a mixture of a chortle and a yodel. Most Basenji noises are usually reserved for moments of happiness and contentment. This is truly something one needs to experience to appreciate!

Upon seeing and smelling the aromatic dash of a rabbit, a Basenji is likely to whimper, and when in pain he can screech like a siren! Also, one should never be fooled into thinking that a Basenji will never disturb the neighbors, because the noises they make can be rather alarming. It is not unknown for police and medical services to have been called to a house because a neighbor thought that someone was in agony inside. Upon arrival, it was discovered that the dreadful noise had emanated from a discontented or excited Basenji!

PHYSICAL CHARACTERISTICS
This is a lightly built and finely boned aristocratic-looking dog, always poised and alert. Compared with body length, the dog appears quite high on his legs. This well-balanced dog, with his definite waist, exhibits gazelle-like grace. The muscular shoulders should be moderately laid back, and, when seen from the front, the Basenji's elbows should be in line with the ribs, the forelegs continuing in a straight line to the ground. The forearms are very long and the pasterns, too, are of good length. The latter should be strong and flexible.

Hindquarters are muscular and they should be strong. In balance with the front assembly, the Basenji has long second thighs, and the stifles are moderately bent. Feet are small and compact, and they have

16–17 inches at the withers, and weighing around 22–24 pounds. Within this fairly narrow size range, bitches are expected to be on the smaller and lighter end of the spectrum and males larger.

The Basenji has a very pliant skin, covered in a coat which requires minimal maintenance as it is short, sleek and close. However, one must not be fooled into thinking that Basenjis do not shed their coats. Some shedding is inevitable, although this breed tends to keep itself as clean as it possibly can, using its own personal grooming methods.

The most commonly seen Basenji color is chestnut red and white, but pure black and white and black, tan and white (tricolor) have also long been recognized. The most recently accepted color is brindle. The American Kennel Club added brindle as the fourth accepted color in 1990, as the color began to be seen more frequently following the importations of the late 1980s. In the UK, however, it was not until 1999 that England's Kennel Club added brindle as an officially accepted color. The color had been seen decades prior and then

The proud head of the Basenji, showing the characteristic wrinkling when ears are pricked.

deep pads with well-arched toes. Nails should be kept short. The same description applies to both the front and hind feet

The head, carried proudly on well-arched neck, is a rather special one. It is well-chiseled and of medium length, tapering toward the nose, with a slight stop. Ears are small, pointed, erect and slightly hooded; when the ears are pricked, fine and profuse wrinkles appear on the forehead. Puppies display more wrinkling than adults, and in tri-colored dogs the wrinkling is less noticeable because of the coloring. The dark, obliquely set, almond-shaped eyes are far-seeing and give a somewhat inscrutable expression.

The Basenji's tail is high set and curls tightly over the spine, lying closely to the thigh in either a single or double curl.

The Basenji is a lightly built, medium-sized dog, standing ideally

The high-set, curled Basenji tail.

resurfaced with the imported dogs from Africa.

The white markings found on a Basenji should be on the feet, chest and tail tips. White legs, a white blaze and a white collar are optional, but the white should not extend beyond the withers. In any color pattern, the distinction between the different colors should be clear.

Occasionally, black hairs can be found on the upper side of the tail of a red and white Basenji, which may seem rather strange. However, this indicates that this particular dog is carrying the genes for tricolor.

A CHILD'S BEST FRIEND

If brought up with children, Basenjis get along extremely well with them. Even if there are no children in the immediate family, it is sensible to introduce your Basenji to your friends' or relatives' children. The devotion will almost inevitably be reciprocal.

Tricolored dogs can be born to two red and white parents, provided they both carry the tricolored gene. However, a black and white Basenji will always have at least one parent of the same color combination.

The red color of the Basenji is much admired when it is of a bright orange-red color, but it may shade to a bright chestnut red or even to a light sandy red.

The Basenji has a typical canine bite, as found in the majority of breeds. The jaw is strong with a perfect, regular scissors bite, the upper teeth closely overlapping the lower ones. Dentition should be complete, and the teeth should be square to the jaws.

BREED-SPECIFIC HEALTH CONSIDERATIONS

All breeds encounter health problems of one sort and another, but Basenji breeders have been most dedicated to health research and eradicating known problems in the breed. As a result, research carried out in different countries has brought various problems to light and this can only be for the future benefit of the breed.

To be forewarned is to be forearmed, so the following section of this chapter is not intended to put fear into those who are considering becoming owners of the breed. Instead I hope that it will enlighten them, so that any health problems encountered can be recognized, guarded against and dealt with as

THE GREAT ESCAPE ARTIST
A great many Basenjis are accomplished escape artists, so beware! Some think nothing of scaling a six-foot fence, and others think chain-link fencing is merely a ladder erected for their convenience. When exercising your Basenji, it is only prudent to keep a careful eye on him!

early as possible, and in the most appropriate manner. Further, the Basenji's Health Research Endowment raises money for continual research into the causes, treatment and prevention of health problems in the breed.

Persistent Pupillary Membrane (PPM)

Shortly before the eyes of a puppy open, a protein is secreted, dissolving the membrane that contains a fine sheet of veins that feed the eye of the puppy in its developmental stages. Sometimes the membrane does not dissolve completely, leaving what are known as PPM strands. They usually look rather like cobwebs, but in bad cases can give the eye a blue hue. A minor case often clears up as the dog matures; in any case, it does not worsen.

PPM is prevalent in Basenjis, although severe cases are now uncommon, thanks to careful breeding. Breeders should have puppies tested and consider PPM status when deciding on dogs to breed.

Fanconi Syndrome

Fanconi syndrome is a deadly disease, especially if not detected in its early stages, and unfortunately it is one of the major health concerns in Basenjis. Fanconi is currently being researched, but generally appears between the ages of four and seven years, although there are exceptions. Owners should begin monthly urine tests when the dog is three years old.

Fanconi is a disease affecting the processing of sugars and proteins. The earliest symptoms are drinking excessive quantities of water, frequent urination and elevated levels of glucose in the urine. The earliest simple check is for sugar in the urine. When glucose is found in the urine, a Basenji is said to be "spilling sugar." It should, though, be borne in mind that a dog with sugar in its urine as well as high blood-sugar levels is likely to be diabetic,

A seven-week-old Basenji, wasting no time in starting to practice the art of escape!

SELF GROOMERS

As Basenjis like to groom themselves, owners should take particular care in selecting safe grooming preparations. The safest are those advertised as being suitable for puppies and for cats. Any other products used should only be considered if they have been recommended as "safe" by Basenji breeders who are already familiar with them.

rather than suffering from Fanconi.

A Fanconi-afflicted dog requires protein, for vital proteins and amino acids are passed out of its body via the urine. Owners with Fanconi-affected Basenjis can help their dogs live normal, or nearly normal, lives, by use of a therapeutic protocol consisting of plenty of fresh water, dietary supplements and blood and urine tests. This necessitates both time and effort on the owner's part, but the disease can be controlled if diagnosed and treated in time. However, Fanconi is an incurable disease and not all Basenjis respond well to the treatment, though thankfully many do. The mode of inheritance is, as yet, unknown, but the disease does appear to occur more frequently in certain lines or families.

HIP DYSPLASIA

Hip dysplasia, although by no means as prevalent in this breed as in others, can crop up. It is a problem involving the malformation of the ball and socket joint at the hip, a developmental condition caused by the interaction of many genes. This results in looseness of the hip joints, and, although not always painful, it can cause lameness, and typical movement can be impaired.

Although a dog's environment does not actually cause hip dysplasia, this may have some bearing on how unstable the hip joint eventually becomes. Osteoarthritis eventually develops as a result of the instability.

Tests for hip dysplasia are available in most countries throughout the world. In the US, hip x-rays are submitted to the Orthopedic Foundation for Animals, and the hips receive a grading that indicates if they are affected or not, and to what degree. The grading also indicates if the dog is or is not suitable for breeding from an HD standpoint.

THYROID PROBLEMS

Hypothyroidism, a hormonal disorder, is common in the breed, Basenjis having a more active thyroid than that of other breeds. If a Basenji's thyroid is underactive for the breed (at an adequately functional level for most other dogs), this can cause both obesity and poor coat condition.

There are many signs of hypothyroidism, and, because these signs can be present in any combination, they may easily be mistaken for other diseases. Classic signs are obesity, hair loss and lethargy, the latter leading to muscle wasting, caused by an inability to get sufficient exercise. In classic cases, the hair loss is bilaterally symmetrical, affecting the same area on both sides of the body, and generally there is no sign of either itching or scratching. Basenjis should be tested for thyroid function. Hypothyroidism is easily treated with supplements; Basenjis also should be routinely tested for auto-immune thyroiditis.

INTESTINAL PROBLEMS

The Basenji can be affected by several types of intestinal problems, some of which are hereditary, some of which are not. One such problem, thought to be inherited, is IPSID (immunoproliferative small intestinal disease), a malabsorption syndrome said to be like Crohn's disease in humans. IPSID is an inflammatory bowel disease with serious consequences. The dog cannot receive proper nutrition from his food, which causes problems in itself, but the disease progresses to weaken the dog's immunological system. In addition to inheritance, allergies, infections and stress also contribute to the onset of IPSID. While IPSID is thought to be inherited, the specifics of its inheritance and onset are not yet known. If left undiagnosed, it can result in death.

While owners take care of their dogs, studies have shown that pet ownership has health benefits for owners, too–not to mention the joys of sharing your life with a one-of-a-kind Basenji!

The symptoms of IPSID are common to many other problems as well: diarrhea, vomiting, appetite and weight changes among them; therefore, a dog must undergo tests to determine if he is affected or if he has a less serious problem. Affected dogs will have low protein levels, but the official diagnosis is done by process of elimination to rule out other diseases. If IPSID is the diagnosis, there are therapeutic and medical measures that allow the dog as long and normal a life as possible, although unfortunately most affected dogs will eventually die of the condition. Treatment includes drug therapy and dietary changes.

While IPSID and related intestinal problems are serious ones, there are many that are not, such as "run-of-the-mill" stomach upset, food allergy, infection, etc. These easily treatable problems present many similar symptoms similar to those presented by the serious problems, which is why veterinary attention and a correct diagnosis is of the utmost importance if your Basenji shows any signs of intestinal problems.

EYE PROBLEMS

Progressive retinal atrophy, usually referred to as PRA, is an inherited eye disorder, not usually discovered until adulthood, in which a dog progressively goes blind. This is often first noticed by night-blindness, but total blindness is unfortunately the inevitable end result. Thankfully, there is no pain.

This used to be only a minor problem in Basenjis, but in recent years has become a cause for greater concern. Research about genetic testing is under way. Breeders have to use their carefully considered knowledge of hereditary factors to avoid, if possible, doubling up on the gene that carries this inherited disease. In most countries, eye tests for PRA are available; with the Basenji, a second opinion is suggested, as tests can turn up false positives and false negatives in the breed.

Another inherited problem is coloboma, in which a portion of the eye is missing. In Basenjis, this usually affects the optic nerve. However, if a dog is diagnosed with coloboma, a second opinion is recommended, as there can be false positives in the breed.

Epithelial/stromal corneal dystrophy causes the cornea to become clouded but does not usually affect a dog's vision. It is believed to be inherited. A more severe and thankfully less common condition is endothelial corneal dystrophy.

All of these eye problems can be detected in an exam from the Canine Eye Registration Foundation (CERF), which is recommended annually for all breeding animals. The annual exam is important, as some of these problems do not present themselves until later in life. This exam also does not determine

---

MORE FROM THE OFA

The Orthopedic Foundation for Animals is not just a registry for hip and elbow dysplasia. In fact, it now offers registries for many hereditary conditions seen in dogs, and is not limited to those of an orthopedic nature. For example, the OFA maintains a cardiac registry, and Basenjis can be tested for heart murmurs and included as normal or affected on the registry. Patellar luxation is a problem with the kneecaps that is common in many breeds of dog, especially smaller breeds. A Basenji can be tested for patellar luxation and his status registered with the OFA. In addition to the conditions mentioned, the OFA tests and maintains registries for Legg-Calve-Perthes disease, thyroid problems, deafness and sebaceous adenitis, and performs DNA testing for a number of other hereditary conditions.

HEAT CYCLES

Unlike other bitches, which experience estrus twice annually, the vast majority of Basenji bitches come into season only once each year, usually in the autumn months. There are exceptions, though these are rare. This is not a health *problem*, just something of which owners should be aware.

whether or not a dog is carrying the gene for a hereditary eye problem. CERF grants certification to animals that test as unaffected, in which case they are cleared for breeding, and the American College of Veterinary Ophthalmologists (ACVO) sets forth breeding recommendations regarding the various eye problems. Dogs with coloboma and endothelial corneal dystrophy will not be granted CERF certification, nor should they be bred according to the ACVO. However, as epithelial corneal dystrophy does not usually compromise vision, an animal thusly affected will receive CERF certification. The ACVO recommends that breeding of animals affected with epithelial corneal dystrophy should be considered by the breeder, but the condition alone does not warrant an animal's exclusion from a breeding program.

Hemolytic Anemia

This is a hereditary problem, passed on by a simple recessive gene, known and researched in the Basenji since the 1960s. A test for carriers was developed; today both DNA and blood tests exist. It is important that the hemolytic anemia status of all breeding dogs is known; either the dog must come from stock that has tested clear (most of today's Basenjis are descended from clear stock) or the dog itself must test clear. The DNA test is very exact, identifying a dog as either affected, a carrier or clear of the gene. In the case of an affected dog, symptoms include low energy levels and possibly fainting, light-colored stools and white gums and mucous membranes. Affected dogs live, at the very most, to be four years of age, although most affected dogs die much earlier.

Umbilical Hernia

An umbilical hernia is seen as a small swelling at the site of the umbilicus, and in Basenjis is often not noticeable until a puppy has reached three or four weeks of age. This is not uncommon in the breed and can be hereditary.

Most hernias are entirely trouble-free, but it is always wise to ask a vet to check the hernia, for sometimes surgical attention is needed. Veterinary attention should be sought if the swelling becomes very red. Owners of pet Basenjis frequently ask the vet to remove the hernia at the time of spaying or neutering, thereby avoiding additional surgery and anesthesia.

INTRODUCTION TO THE BREED STANDARD

The breed standard for the Basenji is approved by the American Kennel Club and, like standards for other breeds, can be changed occasionally. Such changes come about with guidance from experienced people from within the breed clubs who then submit their amended standards to the AKC.

All breed standards are designed effectively to paint a picture in words, though each reader will almost certainly have a slightly different way of interpreting these words. After all, when all is said and done, were everyone to interpret a breed's standard in exactly the same way, there would only be one consistent breed winner at dog shows at any given time!

However familiar you are with the breed, it is always worth refreshing your memory by re-reading the standard, for it is sometimes all too easy to overlook, or perhaps forget,

certain features. A good knowledge of the standard enables owners to absorb as much as possible about this highly individual breed. Hands-on experience, providing an opportunity to assess the structure of dogs, is also always valuable, especially for those who hope ultimately to judge the breed.

A breed standard helps breeders to choose and produce stock that comes as close as possible to the recognized standard, and helps judges to know what they are looking for. This enables judges to make a carefully considered decision when selecting the most typical Basenji present to head their line of winners.

In any event, to fully comprehend the intricacies of a breed, reading words alone is never enough. In addition, it is essential for devotees to watch the Basenji classes being judged at shows and, if possible, to attend seminars at which the breed is discussed.

THE AMERICAN KENNEL CLUB BREED STANDARD FOR THE BASENJI

General Appearance: The Basenji is a small, short haired hunting dog from Africa. It is short backed and lightly built, appearing high on the leg compared to its length. The wrinkled head is proudly carried on a well arched neck and the tail is set high and curled. Elegant and graceful, the whole demeanor is one of poise and inquiring alertness. The balanced structure and the smooth musculature enables it to move with ease and agility. The Basenji hunts by both sight and scent. *Characteristics*—The Basenji should not bark but is not mute. The wrinkled forehead, tightly curled tail and swift, effortless gait (resembling a racehorse trotting full out) are typical of the breed. *Faults*—Any departure from the following points must be considered a fault, and the seriousness with which the fault is regarded is to be in exact proportion to its degree.

Size, Proportion, Substance: Ideal height for dogs is 17 inches and bitches 16 inches. Dogs 17 inches and bitches 16 inches from front of chest to point of buttocks. Approximate weight for dogs, 24 pounds and bitches, 22 pounds. Lightly built within this height to weight ratio.

MEETING THE IDEAL

The American Kennel Club defines a standard as: "A description of the ideal dog of each recognized breed, to serve as an ideal against which dogs are judged at shows." This "blueprint" is drawn up by the breed's recognized parent club, approved by a majority of its membership and then submitted to the AKC for approval. Standards are handled differently in different countries. In England, for example, all standards and changes are controlled by The Kennel Club.

The AKC states that "An understanding of any breed must begin with its standard. This applies to all dogs, not just those intended for showing." The picture that the standard draws of the dog's type, gait, temperament and structure is the guiding image used by breeders as they plan their programs.

Head: The head is proudly carried. *Eyes*—Dark hazel to dark brown, almond shaped, obliquely set and farseeing. Rims dark. *Ears*—Small, erect and slightly hooded, of fine texture and set well forward on top of head. The skull is flat, well chiseled and of medium width, tapering toward the eyes. The foreface tapers from eye to muzzle with a perceptible stop. Muzzle shorter than skull, neither coarse nor snipy, but with rounded cushions. Wrinkles appear upon the forehead when ears are erect, and are fine and profuse. Side wrinkles are desirable, but should never be exaggerated into dewlap.

Wrinkles are most noticeable in puppies, and because of lack of shadowing, less noticeable in blacks, tricolors and brindles. *Nose*—Black greatly desired. *Teeth*—Evenly aligned with a scissors bite.

Neck, Topline, Body: Neck of good length, well crested and slightly full at base of throat. Well set into shoulders. *Topline*—Back level. *Body*—Balanced with a short back, short coupled and ending in a definite waist. Ribs moderately sprung, deep to elbows and oval. Slight forechest in front of point of shoulder. Chest of medium width. *Tail* is

A beautiful Basenji head, wrinkles and all! The pricked ears and wrinkling contribute to the breed's look of alertness and intelligence.

Desirable head, flat, well chiseled
and of medium width.

Correct ears, dark eyes and good
wrinkling.

Ears too large and wide set;
light eyes; lack of wrinkling.

Desirable body, balanced with short, level
back and strong fore- and rear quarters.

Lacking angulation in front and
rear; lack of depth in chest.

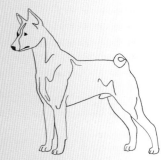

Thick, loaded shoulders,
undesirable.

Good tail (double curl).

Good tail (single curl).

Fair tail (loose curl).

Poor tail (no curl).

set high on topline, bends acutely forward and lies well curled over to either side.

Forequarters: Shoulders moderately laid back. Shoulder blade and upper arm of approximately equal length. Elbows tucked firmly against brisket. Legs straight with clean fine bone, long forearm and well defined sinews. Pasterns of good length, strong and flexible. *Feet*—Small, oval and compact with thick pads and well arched toes. Dewclaws are usually removed.

Hindquarters: Medium width, strong and muscular, hocks well let down and turned neither in nor out, with long second thighs and moderately bent stifles. *Feet*—Same as in "Forequarters."

Coat and Color: Coat short and fine. Skin very pliant. *Color*—Chestnut red; pure black; tricolor (pure black and chestnut red); or brindle (black stripes on a background of chestnut red); all with white feet, chest and tail tip. White legs, blaze and collar optional. The amount of white should never predominate over primary color. Color and markings should be rich, clear and well-defined, with a distinct line of demarcation between the black and red of tricolors and the stripes of brindles.

Gait: Swift, tireless trot. Stride is long, smooth, effortless and the topline remains level. Coming and going, the straight column of bones from shoulder joint to foot and from hip joint to pad remains unbroken, converging toward the centerline under the body. The faster the trot, the greater the convergence.

Temperament: An intelligent, independent, but affectionate and alert breed. Can be aloof with strangers.

**Approved May 8, 1990
Effective June 28, 1990**

BASENJI

HOW TO SELECT A PUPPY

Before reaching the decision that you will definitely look for a Basenji puppy, it is essential that you are fully clear in your mind that this is the most suitable breed for you and for your family. There is no disputing the fact that this is a very special breed, and all the pros and cons must be carefully weighed against each other before reaching the important decision to acquire a Basenji.

When considering your decision, you must also ask yourself why you want a Basenji—purely as a pet or as a show dog? This should be made clear to the breeder when you make your initial inquiries, for you will certainly need to take the breeder's advice as to which available puppy shows the most promise for the show ring. If looking for a pet, you should discuss your family situation with the breeder and take his advice as to which puppy is likely to suit best in lifestyle and personality.

Often it is wisest not to select either the most dominant or the most docile puppy in a litter.

> **COST OF OWNERSHIP**
> The purchase price of your puppy is merely the first expense in the typical dog budget. Quality dog food, veterinary care (sickness and health maintenance), dog supplies and grooming costs will add up to big bucks every year. Can you adequately afford to support a canine addition to the family?

Watch the puppies interact together, and with the breeder's adult Basenjis too. An emotionally stable puppy will not avoid adult dogs, but will defer to them. A Basenji with a stable temperament

A good breeder will be eager for you to meet all of the Basenjis on the premises to help you learn more about the dogs of her line.

A SHOW PUPPY

If you plan to show your puppy, you must first deal with a reputable breeder who shows his dogs and has had some success in the conformation ring. The puppy's pedigree should include one or more champions in the first and second generation. You should be familiar with the breed and breed standard so you can know what qualities to look for in your puppy. The breeder's observations and recommendations also are invaluable aids in selecting your future champion. If you consider an older puppy, be sure that the puppy has been properly socialized with people and not isolated in a kennel without substantial daily human contact.

as such a dog is likely to have serious problems in socializing.

You should have done plenty of background "homework" on the breed, and preferably have visited a few shows at which there were classes for the Basenji, giving you an opportunity to see the breed in some numbers. This will also have provided you with the opportunity to see the dogs with their breeders and owners.

Ideally the Basenji that you select should remain with you for the duration of its life, which is usually around 12 or more years, so making the right decision from the outset is of the utmost importance. No dog should be moved from one home to another simply because his owners were not considerate enough to have done sufficient background research before selecting the breed. It is always important to remember when looking for a puppy that a good breeder will be assessing you as a prospective new owner just as carefully as you are selecting the breeder.

Puppies almost invariably look enchanting, but you must select one from a caring breeder who has given the puppies all the attention they deserve and has looked after them well. It is important for breeders to socialize Basenji puppies as early as possible, and it should be apparent when you meet the litter that this has been done.

The puppy you select should

should also not lunge out and try to attack each and every thing that passes. However, never be tempted to take pity on an unduly shy puppy. In doing so, you will be asking for trouble in the long term,

FINDING A QUALIFIED BREEDER

Before you begin your puppy search, ask for references from your veterinarian and perhaps other breeders to refer you to someone they believe is reputable. Responsible breeders usually raise only one or two breeds of dog. Avoid any breeder who has several different breeds or has several litters at the same time. Dedicated breeders are usually involved in the national breed club. Many participate in some activity related to their breed. Just as you want to be assured of the breeder's qualifications, the breeder wants to be assured that you will make a worthy owner. Expect the breeder to interview you, asking questions about your goals for the pup, your experience with dogs and what kind of home you will provide.

look well fed, but not pot-bellied, as this might indicate worms. Eyes should look bright and clear, without discharge. The nose should be moist, an indication of good health, but should never be runny; it is also important that there is no evidence of loose bowels or of parasites. His teeth and mouth should be healthy and indicative of a correct bite. The puppy you choose should also have a healthy-looking coat, an important indicator of good health internally.

You might consider the sex of your puppy as well before you begin visiting litters. Males are generally larger, though not always. Males tend to be sensitive about being approached by other males and become annoyed when other males approach those they consider "their" females. However, two males brought up together, without females around, often get on well together. Bitches can be dominant with both other dogs and with people; it is often not easy to keep bitches together.

A COMMITTED NEW OWNER

By now you should understand what makes the Basenji a most unique and special dog, one that may fit nicely into your family and lifestyle. If you have researched breeders, you should be able to recognize a knowledgeable and responsible Basenji breeder who cares not only about his pups but also about what kind of owner you

Snuggling up! The Basenji pup will welcome a soft and cozy place of his own.

If you have completed the final step in your new journey, you have found a litter, or possibly two, of quality Basenji pups. A visit with the puppies and their breeder should be an education in itself. Breed research, breeder selection and puppy visitation are very important aspects of finding the puppy of your dreams. Beyond that, these things also lay the foundation for a successful future with your pup. Personalities within each litter vary, from the shy and easygoing puppy to the one who is dominant and assertive, with most pups falling somewhere in between. Basenji pups may not be as outgoing as pups of other breeds, like Golden Retrievers or Collies, so do not expect young Basenjis to be overly demonstrative.

By spending time with the puppies, you will be able to recognize certain behaviors and what these behaviors indicate about each pup's temperament. Which type of pup will comple-ment your family dynamics is best determined by observing the puppies in action within their "pack." Your breeder's expertise and recommendations are very valuable. Although you may fall in love with a bold and brassy male, the breeder may suggest that another pup would be best for you. The breeder's experience in rearing Basenji pups and matching their temperaments with appropriate humans offers the best assurance

PEDIGREE VS. REGISTRATION CERTIFICATE

Too often new owners are confused between these two important documents. Your puppy's pedigree, essentially a family tree, is a written record of a dog's genealogy of three generations or more. The pedigree will show you the names as well as performance titles of all dogs in your pup's background. Your breeder must provide you with a registration application, with his part properly filled out. You must complete the application and send it to the AKC with the proper fee. Every puppy must come from a litter that has been AKC-registered by the breeder, born in the US and from a sire and dam that are also registered with the AKC.

The seller must provide you with complete records to identify the puppy. The AKC requires that the seller provide the buyer with the following: breed; sex, color and markings; date of birth; litter number (when available); names and registration numbers of the parents; breeder's name; and date sold or delivered.

will be. The Basenji Club of America (www.basenji.org) should be your source for breeder referrals, as their member breeders are obliged to uphold strict ethical breeding practices for the better-ment of the breed.

THE FAMILY TREE

Your puppy's pedigree is his family tree. Just as a child may resemble his parents and grandparents, so too will a puppy reflect the qualities, good and bad, of his ancestors, especially those in the first two generations. Therefore it's important to know as much as possible about a puppy's immediate relatives. Reputable and experienced breeders should be able to explain the pedigree and why they chose to breed from the particular dogs they used.

that your pup will meet your needs and expectations. The type of puppy that you select is just as important as your decision that the Basenji is the breed for you.

The decision to live with a Basenji is a serious commitment and not one to be taken lightly. This puppy is a living sentient being that will be dependent on you for basic survival for his entire life. Beyond the basics of survival—food, water, shelter and protection—he needs much, much more. The new pup needs love, nurturing and a proper canine education to mold him into a responsible, well-behaved canine citizen. Your Basenji's health and good manners will need consistent monitoring and regular "tune-ups," so your job as a responsible dog owner will be ongoing throughout every stage of his life. If you are not

prepared to accept these responsibilities and commit to them for the next decade, likely longer, then you are not prepared to own a dog of any breed.

Although the responsibilities of owning a dog may at times tax your patience, the joy of living with your Basenji far outweighs the workload, and a well-mannered adult dog is worth your time and effort. Before your very eyes, your new charge will grow up to be your most loyal friend, devoted to you unconditionally.

YOUR BASENJI SHOPPING LIST

Just as expectant parents prepare a nursery for their baby, so should you ready your home for the arrival of your Basenji pup. If you have the necessary puppy supplies purchased and in place before he comes home, it will ease the puppy's transition from the warmth and familiarity of his mom and littermates to the brand-new environment of his new home and

A ventilated soft-sided doggie "tote" can be used to transport a Basenji pup.

human family. You will be too busy to stock up and prepare your house after your pup comes home, that's for sure! Imagine how a pup must feel upon being transported to a strange new place. It's up to you to comfort him and to let your little pup know that he is going to be happy with you.

FOOD AND WATER BOWLS

Your puppy will need separate bowls for his food and water. Stainless steel pans are generally preferred over plastic bowls since they sterilize better and pups are less inclined to chew on the metal. Heavy-duty ceramic bowls are popular, but consider how often you will have to pick up those heavy bowls. Buy adult-sized pans, as your puppy will soon grow into them.

THE DOG CRATE

If you think that crates are tools of punishment and confinement for when a dog has misbehaved, think

Always curious and always ready to chew, the Basenji pup needs close supervision to keep him safe.

> ## MAKE A COMMITMENT
> Dogs are most assuredly man's best friend, but they are also a lot of work. When you add a puppy to your family, you also are adding to your daily responsibilities for years to come. Dogs need more than just food, water and a place to sleep. They also require training (which can be ongoing throughout the lifetime of the dog), activity to keep them physically and mentally fit and hands-on attention every day, plus grooming and health care. Your life as you now know it may well disappear! Are you prepared for such drastic changes?

again. Most breeders and almost all trainers recommend a crate as the preferred house-training aid as well as for all-around puppy training and safety. Because dogs are natural den creatures that prefer cave-like environments, the benefits of crate use are many. The crate provides the puppy with his very own "safe house," a cozy place to sleep, take a break or seek comfort with a favorite toy; a travel aid to house your dog when on the road, at motels or at the vet's office; a training aid to help teach your puppy proper toileting habits; a place of solitude when non-dog people happen to drop by and don't want a lively puppy—or even a well-behaved adult dog—saying hello or begging for attention.

Crates come in several types, although the wire crate and the fiberglass airline-type crate are the most popular. Basenjis, being the alert and curious creatures they are, prefer the wire crate because they like to know and see everything going on around them. Wire crates also offer more air flow, which is ideal for any dog. Many of the wire crates easily fold down for easy transport. The fiberglass crates, similar to those used by the airlines for animal transport, are sturdier and often used for travel crates. However, the fiberglass crates do not fold and are less ventilated than a wire crate, which can be problematic in hot weather. Some of the newer crates are made of heavy plastic mesh; they are very lightweight and fold up into slim-line suitcases. However, a mesh crate might not be suitable for a

Your Basenji will enjoy outdoor excursions, such as hiking and strolls through the countryside, on leash and with his favorite person.

pup with manic chewing habits.

Don't bother with a puppy-sized crate. Although your Basenji will be a wee fellow when you bring him home, he will grow up in the blink of an eye and your puppy crate will be useless. Purchase a crate that will accommodate an adult Basenji. He will stand about 17 inches when fully grown. A medium-sized wire crate, measuring 30 inches long by 21 inches wide by 24 inches high, will be comfortable for use in the home. The same crate or one slightly smaller can be used as a travel crate.

The three most common crate types: mesh (left), wire (right) and fiberglass (top).

CRATE EXPECTATIONS

To make the crate more inviting to your puppy, you can offer his first meal or two inside the crate, always keeping the crate door open so that he does not feel confined. Keep a favorite toy or two in the crate for him to play with while inside. You can also cover the crate at night with a lightweight sheet to make it more den-like and remove the stimuli of household activity. Never put him into his crate as punishment or as you are scolding him, since he will then associate his crate with negative situations and avoid going there.

BEDDING AND CRATE PADS

Your Basenji puppy will enjoy some type of soft bedding in his "room" (the crate), something he can snuggle into to feel cozy and secure. Old towels or blankets are good choices for a young pup, since he may (and probably will) have a toileting accident or two in the crate or decide to chew on the bedding material. Once he is fully trained and out of the early chewing stage, you can replace the puppy bedding with a permanent crate pad if you prefer. Crate pads and other dog beds run the gamut from inexpensive to high-end doggie-designer styles, but don't splurge on the good stuff until you are sure that your Basenji puppy is reliable and won't tear it up or make a mess on it.

PUPPY TOYS

Just as infants and older children require objects to stimulate their minds and bodies, puppies need toys to entertain their curious brains, wiggly paws and achy teeth. A fun array of safe doggie toys will help satisfy your puppy's chewing instincts and distract him from gnawing on the leg of your antique chair or your new leather sofa. Most puppy toys are cute and look as if they would be a lot of fun, but not all are necessarily safe or good for your puppy, so use caution when you go puppy-toy shopping.

Basenjis are great chewers and the provision of safe chew toys gives them much enjoyment. The best "chewcifiers" are sturdy nylon and hard rubber bones, which are safe to gnaw on and come in sizes appropriate for all age groups and breeds. Be especially careful of natural bones which can splinter or develop dangerous sharp edges; pups can easily swallow or choke on those bone splinters. Veterinarians often tell of surgical nightmares involving bits of splintered bone, because in addition to the danger of choking, the sharp pieces can damage the intestinal tract.

Similarly, rawhide chews, while a favorite of most dogs and puppies, can be equally dangerous. Pieces of rawhide are easily swallowed after they get soft and gummy from chewing, and dogs have been known to choke on large

This Basenji pup has some growing to do to fill his crate! During crate-training, the crate can be partitioned and the pup given more room as he grows.

Wire pens should be used with caution with Basenjis, who are easily able to climb out of this type of enclosure.

pieces of ingested rawhide. Rawhide chews should be offered only when you can supervise the puppy.

Soft woolly toys are special puppy favorites. They come in a wide variety of cute shapes and sizes; some look like little stuffed animals. Puppies love to shake them up and toss them about, or simply carry them around. Be careful of fuzzy toys that have button eyes or noses that your pup could chew off and swallow, and make sure that he does not ingest the stuffing or disembowel a squeaky toy to remove the squeaker! Braided rope toys are similar in that they are fun to chew and toss around, but they shred easily and the strings are easy to swallow. The strings are not

digestible and, if the puppy doesn't pass them in his stool, he could end up at the vet's office. As with rawhides, your puppy should be closely monitored with rope toys.

CONFINEMENT

It is wise to keep your puppy confined to a small "puppy-proofed" area of the house for his first few weeks at home. If he is allowed to roam through the entire house or even only several rooms, it will be more difficult to house-train him. Often owners rely on baby gates to partition a room to help keep the dog in a particular area of the house. For the Basenji, baby gates are amusing objects to climb upon and will not serve the desired purpose, though they are great exercise!

If you believe that your pup has ingested a piece of one of his toys, check his stools for the next couple of days to see if he passes the item when he defecates. At the same time, also watch for signs of intestinal distress. A call to your veterinarian might be in order to get his advice and be on the safe side.

An all-time favorite toy for puppies (young and old!) is the empty gallon milk jug. Hard plastic juice containers—46 ounces or more—are also excellent. Such containers make lots of noise when they are batted about, and puppies go crazy with delight as they play with them. However, they don't often last very long, so be sure to remove and replace them when they get chewed up.

A word of caution about homemade toys: be careful with your choices of non-traditional play objects. Never use old shoes or socks, since a puppy cannot distinguish between the old ones on which he's allowed to chew and the new ones in your closet that are strictly off limits. That principle

TOYS 'R SAFE

The vast array of tantalizing puppy toys is staggering. Stroll through any pet shop or pet-supply outlet and you will see that the choices can be overwhelming. However, not all dog toys are safe or sensible. Most very young puppies enjoy soft woolly toys that they can snuggle with and carry around. (You know they have outgrown them when they shred them up!) Avoid toys that have buttons, tabs or other enhancements that can be chewed off and swallowed. Soft toys that squeak are fun, but make sure your puppy does not disembowel the toy and remove (and swallow) the squeaker. Toys that rattle or make noise can excite a puppy, but they present the same danger as the squeaky kind and so require supervision. Hard rubber toys that bounce can also entertain a pup, but make sure that the toy is too big for your pup to swallow.

Comfortable in his crate, this Basenji appreciates his own den-like space.

TEETHING TIME

All puppies chew. It's normal canine behavior. Chewing just plain feels good to a puppy, especially during the three- to five-month teething period when the adult teeth are breaking through the gums. Rather than attempting to eliminate such a strong natural chewing instinct, you will be more successful if you redirect it and teach your puppy what he may or may not chew. Correct inappropriate chewing with a sharp "No!" and offer him a chew toy, praising him when he takes it. Don't become discouraged. Chewing usually decreases after the adult teeth have come in.

applies to anything that resembles something that you don't want your puppy to chew up.

COLLARS

A lightweight nylon collar is the best choice for a very young pup. Quick-clip collars are easy to put on and remove, and they can be adjusted as the puppy grows. Introduce him to his collar as soon as he comes home to get him accustomed to wearing it. He'll get used to it quickly and won't mind a bit. Make sure that it is snug enough that it won't slip off, yet loose enough to be comfortable for the pup. You should be able to slip two fingers between the collar and his neck. Check the collar often, as puppies grow in spurts, and his collar can become too tight almost overnight. Choke collars for training are not a good choice, as forceful training methods are not suitable for the Basenji and it is recommended to use a gentler type of training collar, like a head collar, if a training collar is needed.

LEASHES

A 6-foot nylon lead is an excellent choice for a young puppy. It is lightweight and not as tempting to chew as a leather lead. You can switch to a 6-foot leather lead after your pup has grown and is used to walking politely on a lead. For initial puppy walks and house-training purposes, you should invest in a shorter lead so that you have more control over the puppy. At first, you don't want him wandering too far away from you, and when taking him out for toileting you will want to keep him in the specific area chosen for his potty spot.

Once the puppy is heel-trained with a traditional leash, you can consider purchasing a retractable lead. This type of lead is excellent for walking adult dogs that are

Collaring Our Canines

The standard flat collar with a buckle or a snap, in leather, nylon or cotton, is widely regarded as the everyday all-purpose collar. If the collar fits correctly, you should be able to fit two fingers between the collar and the dog's neck.

Leather Buckle Collars

The martingale, Greyhound or limited-slip collar is preferred by many dog owners and trainers. It is fixed with an extra loop that tightens when pressure is applied to the leash. The martingale collar gets tighter but does not "choke" the dog. The limited-slip collar should only be used for walking and training, not for free play or interaction with another dog. These types of collar should never be left on the dog, as the extra loop can lead to accidents.

Limited-Slip Collar

Choke collars, usually made of stainless steel, are made for training purposes but are not recommended for every breed. The chains can injure small dogs or damage long/abundant coats, and are considered too harsh for certain breeds. Thin nylon choke leads are commonly used on show dogs while in the ring, though they are not practical for everyday use.

The harness, with two or three straps that attach over the dog's shoulders and around his torso, is a humane and safe alternative to the conventional collar. By and large, a well-made harness is virtually escape-proof. Harnesses are available in nylon and mesh and can be outfitted on most dogs, with chest girths ranging from 10 to 30 inches.

Snap Bolt Choke Collar

Harness

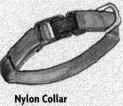

Nylon Collar

Quick-Click Closure

Snake Chain · **Chrome Steel** · **Fur-Saver**

Choke Chain Collars

A head collar, composed of a nylon strap that goes around the dog's muzzle and a second strap that wraps around his neck, offers the owner better control over his dog. This device is recommended for problem-solving with dogs (including jumping up, pulling and aggressive behaviors), but must be used with care.

A training halter, including a flat collar and two straps, made of nylon and webbing, is designed for walking. There are several on the market; some are more difficult to put on the dog than others. The halter harness, with two small slip rings at each end, is recommended for ease of use.

already leash-wise. The retractable lead allows the dog to roam farther away from you and explore a wider area when out walking, and also retracts when you need to keep him close to you.

HOME SAFETY FOR YOUR PUPPY

The importance of puppy-proofing cannot be overstated. In addition to making your house comfortable for your Basenji's arrival, you also must make sure that your house is safe for your puppy before you bring him home. There are countless hazards in the owner's personal living environment that a pup can sniff, chew, swallow or destroy, and a Basenji's curiousity is insatiable! Many of these dangers are obvious; others are not. Do a thorough advance house check to remove or rearrange those things that could hurt your puppy, keeping any potentially dangerous items out of areas to which he will have access.

Electrical cords are especially dangerous, since puppies view them as irresistible chew toys. Unplug and remove all exposed cords or fasten them beneath a baseboard where the puppy cannot reach them. Veterinarians and firefighters can tell you horror stories about electrical burns and house fires that resulted from puppy-chewed electrical cords. Consider this a most serious precaution for your puppy and the

---

FIRST CAR RIDE

The ride to your home from the breeder will no doubt be your puppy's first automobile experience, and you should make every effort to keep him comfortable and secure. Bring a large towel or small blanket for the puppy to lie on during the trip and an extra towel in case the pup gets carsick or has a potty accident. It's best to have another person with you to hold the puppy in his lap. Most puppies will fall fast asleep from the rolling motion of the car. If the ride is lengthy, you may have to stop so that the puppy can relieve himself, so be sure to bring a leash and collar for those stops. Avoid rest areas for potty trips, since those are frequented by many dogs, who may carry parasites or disease. It's better to stop at grassy areas near gas stations or shopping centers to prevent unhealthy exposure for your pup.

---

rest of your family.

Scout your home for tiny objects that might be seen at a pup's eye level. Keep medication bottles and cleaning supplies well out of reach, and do the same with waste baskets and other trash containers. It goes without saying that you should not use rodent poison or other toxic chemicals in any puppy area and that you must keep such containers safely locked up. You will be amazed at how many places a curious puppy can discover!

Leash Life

Dogs love leashes! Believe it or not, most dogs dance for joy every time their owners pick up their leashes. The leash means that the dog is going for a walk—and there are few things more exciting than that! Here are some of the kinds of leashes that are commercially available.

Nylon Leash

Leather Leash

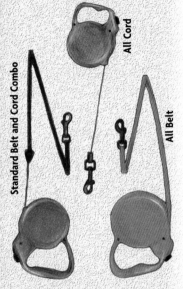

Standard Belt and Cord Combo

All Cord

All Belt

Retractable Leashes

Traditional Leash: Made of cotton, nylon or leather, these leashes are usually about 6 feet in length. A quality-made leather leash is softer on the hands than a nylon one. Durable woven cotton is a popular option. Lengths can vary up to about 48 feet, designed for different uses.

Chain Leash: Usually a metal chain leash with a plastic handle. This is not the best choice for most breeds, as it is heavier than other leashes and difficult to manage.

Retractable Leash: A long nylon cord is housed in a plastic device for extending and retracting. This leash is ideal for taking trained dogs for long walks in open areas, although it is not always suitable for large, powerful breeds. Different lengths and sizes are available, so check that you purchase one appropriate for your dog's weight.

Elastic Leash: A nylon leash with an elastic extension. This is useful for well-trained dogs, especially in conjunction with a head halter.

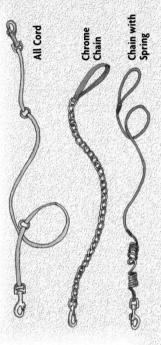

All Cord

Chrome Chain

Chain with Spring

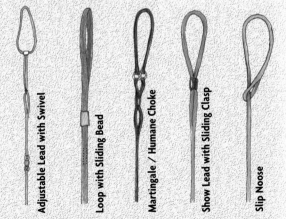

Adjustable Lead with Swivel

Loop with Sliding Bead

Martingale / Humane Choke

Show Lead with Sliding Clasp

Slip Noose

A Variety of Collar-and-Leash-in-One Products

Avoid leashes that are completely elastic, as they afford minimal control to the handler.

Adjustable Leash: This has two snaps, one on each end, and several metal rings. It is handy if you need to tether your dog temporarily, but is never to be used with a choke collar.

Tab Leash: A short leash (4 to 6 inches long) that attaches to your dog's collar. This device serves like a handle, in case you have to grab your dog while he's exercising off lead. It's ideal for "half-trained" dogs or dogs that listen only half of the time.

Slip Leash: Essentially a leash with a collar built in, similar to what a dog-show handler uses to show a dog. This British-style collar has a ring on the end so that you can form a slip collar. Useful if you have to catch your own runaway dog or a stray.

Once your house has cleared inspection, check your yard. The yard should be enclosed by a sturdy fence, well embedded into the ground and of sufficient height. However, don't let a fence give you a false sense of security, especially with the professional-climbing Basenji! You would also be surprised at how crafty (and persistent) a dog can be in figuring out how to dig under and squeeze his way through small holes. The author recommends a privacy-type fence, not a chain-link fence (a.k.a.,

TOXIC PLANTS

Plants are natural Basenji magnets, but many can be harmful, even fatal, if ingested by a puppy or adult dog. Digging up and eating plants is a favorite pastime of some Basenjis. Scout your yard and home interior and remove any plants, bushes or flowers that could be even mildly dangerous. It could save your puppy's life. You can obtain a complete list of toxic plants from your vet, at the public library or by looking online.

a ladder for the Basenji!). It must be high enough and deep enough into the ground to contain the dog. Basenjis have been known to climb over a 6-foot-high fence, so close supervision also is necessary. Check the fence periodically for necessary repairs. If there is a weak link or space to squeeze through, you can be sure a determined Basenji will discover it.

The garage and shed can be hazardous places for a pup, as things like fertilizers, chemicals and tools are usually kept there. It's best to keep these areas off limits to the pup. Antifreeze is especially dangerous to dogs, as they find the taste appealing and it takes only a few licks from the driveway to kill a dog, puppy or adult, small breed or large.

VISITING THE VETERINARIAN

A good vet with knowledge of the Basenji's particular health concerns is your puppy's best health-insurance policy. If you do not already have a vet, ask your breeder and experienced dog people in your area for recommendations so that you can select a vet before you bring your Basenji puppy home. Also arrange for your puppy's first veterinary examination beforehand, since many vets don't always have appointments available immediately and your puppy should visit the vet within a day or so of coming home.

It's important to make sure

A Dog-Safe Home

The dog-safety police are taking you and your new puppy on a house tour. Let's go room by room and see how safe your own home is for your new pup. The following items are doggie dangers, so either they must be removed or the dog should be monitored or not allowed access to these areas.

Living Room

- house plants (some varieties are poisonous)
- fireplace or wood-burning stove
- paint on the walls (lead-based paint is toxic)
- lead drapery weights (toxic lead)
- lamps and electrical cords
- carpet cleaners or deodorizers

Outdoors

- swimming pool
- pesticides
- toxic plants
- lawn fertilizers

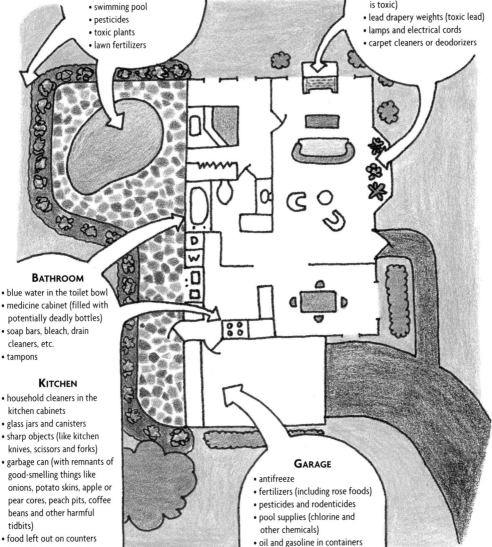

Bathroom

- blue water in the toilet bowl
- medicine cabinet (filled with potentially deadly bottles)
- soap bars, bleach, drain cleaners, etc.
- tampons

Kitchen

- household cleaners in the kitchen cabinets
- glass jars and canisters
- sharp objects (like kitchen knives, scissors and forks)
- garbage can (with remnants of good-smelling things like onions, potato skins, apple or pear cores, peach pits, coffee beans and other harmful tidbits)
- food left out on counters (some foods are toxic to dogs)

Garage

- antifreeze
- fertilizers (including rose foods)
- pesticides and rodenticides
- pool supplies (chlorine and other chemicals)
- oil and gasoline in containers
- sharp objects, electrical cords and power tools

Having your new Basenji pup checked by a vet should be one of the first things you do.

breeder. Your vet is a great source of canine health information, so be sure to ask questions and take notes. Creating a health journal for your puppy will make a handy reference for his wellness and any future health problems that may arise.

MEETING THE FAMILY
Your Basenji's homecoming is an exciting time for all members of the family, and it's only natural that everyone will be eager to meet him, pet him and play with him. However, for the puppy's sake, it's best to make these initial family

your puppy's first visit to the vet is a pleasant and positive one. The vet should take great care to befriend the pup and handle him gently to make their first meeting a positive experience. The vet will give the pup a thorough physical examination and set up a schedule for vaccinations and other necessary wellness visits. Be sure to show your vet any health and inoculation records, which you should have received from your

ASK THE VET
Help your vet help you to become a well-informed dog owner. Don't be shy about becoming involved in your puppy's veterinary care by asking questions and gaining as much knowledge as you can. For starters, ask what shots your puppy is getting and what diseases they prevent, and discuss with your vet the safest way to vaccinate. Find out what is involved in your dog's annual wellness visits. If you plan to spay or neuter, discuss the best age at which to have this done. Discuss the particular problems that can occur in the Basenji. Start out on the right "paw" with your puppy's vet and develop good communication with him, as he will care for your dog's health throughout the dog's entire life.

meetings as uneventful as possible. The last thing you want to do is smother him, as Basenjis are not particularly cuddly dogs and too much too soon will only frighten him further. Give him time to warm up to his hew family.

Remember, your pup has just left his dam and his littermates and is away from the breeder's home for the first time. He is apprehensive and wondering where he is and who all these strange humans are. It's best to let him explore on his own and meet the family members as he feels comfortable. Let him investigate all the new smells, sights and sounds at his own pace. Children should be especially careful to not get overly excited, use loud voices or hug the pup too tightly. Be calm, attentive and affectionate, gently forming a bond and being ready to comfort him if he appears frightened or uneasy.

Be sure to show your puppy his new crate during this first day home. Toss a treat or two inside the crate; if he associates the crate with food, he will associate the crate with good things. If he is comfortable with the crate, you can offer him his first meal inside it. Leave the door ajar so he can wander in and out as he chooses.

FIRST NIGHT IN HIS NEW HOME

So much has happened in your Basenji puppy's first day away from the breeder. He's had his first car ride to his new home. He's met his

THE GRASS IS ALWAYS GREENER

Must dog owners decide between their beloved canine pals and their perfectly manicured emerald-green lawns? Just as dog urine is no tonic for growing grass, lawn chemicals are extremely dangerous to your dog. Fertilizers, pesticides and herbicides pose real threats to canines and humans alike. Dogs should be kept off treated grounds for at least 24 hours following treatment. Consider some organic options for your lawn care, such as using a homemade compost or a natural fertilizer instead of a commercial chemical. Some dog-conscious lawnkeepers avoid fertilizers entirely, keeping up their lawns by watering, aerating, mowing and seeding frequently.

As always, dogs complicate the equation. Canines love grass. They roll in it, eat it and love to bury their noses in it—and then do their business in it! Grass can mean hours of feel-good, smell-good fun! In addition to the dangers of lawn-care chemicals, there's also the threat of burs, thorns and pebbles in the grass, not to mention the very common grass allergy. Many dogs develop an incurably itchy skin condition from grass, especially in the late summer when the world is in full bloom.

with his littermates, and those familiar scents are a great comfort for the puppy on his first night without his siblings.

He will probably whine or cry. The puppy is objecting to the confinement and the fact that he is alone for the first time. This can be a stressful time for you as well as for the pup. It's important that you remain strong and don't let the puppy out of his crate to comfort him. He will fall asleep eventually. If you release him, the puppy will learn that crying means "out" and will continue that habit. You are

new human family and perhaps the other family pets. He has explored his new house and yard, at least those places where he is to be allowed during his first weeks at home. He may have visited his new veterinarian. He has eaten his first meal or two away from his dam and littermates. Surely that's enough to tire out an eight-week-old Basenji pup...or so you hope!

It's bedtime. During the day, the pup investigated his crate, which is his new den and sleeping space, so it is not entirely strange to him. Line the crate with a soft towel or blanket that he can snuggle into and gently place him into the crate for the night. Some breeders send home a piece of bedding from where the pup slept

---

THE FAMILY FELINE

The Basenji has cat-like traits, but how will he get along with the family cat? A resident cat has feline squatter's rights. The cat will treat the newcomer (your puppy) as she sees fit, regardless of what you do or say. So it's best to let the two of them work things out on their own terms. Cats have a height advantage and will generally leap to higher ground to avoid direct contact with a rambunctious pup. Some will hiss and boldly swat at a pup who passes by or tries to reach the cat. Keep the puppy under control in the presence of the cat and they will eventually become accustomed to each other.

Here's a hint: move the cat's litter box where the puppy can't get into it! It's best to do so well before the pup comes home so the cat is used to the new location.

laying the groundwork for future habits. Some breeders find that soft music can soothe a crying pup and help him get to sleep.

SOCIALIZING YOUR PUPPY

The first 20 weeks of your Basenji puppy's life are the most important of his entire lifetime. A properly socialized puppy will grow up to be a confident and stable adult who will be a pleasure to live with and a welcome addition to the family. The importance of socialization cannot be overemphasized, especially with a breed that tends to be aloof. Research on canine behavior has proven that puppies who are not exposed to new sights, sounds, people and animals during their first 20 weeks of life will grow up to be timid and fearful, even aggressive, and unable to flourish outside their home environment.

Socializing your puppy will be a fun time for you both. Lead training goes hand in hand with socialization, so your puppy will be learning how to walk on a lead at the same time that he's meeting the neighborhood. Because the Basenji is such an intriguing breed, most everyone will be interested in meeting "the new kid on the block." Take him for short walks, to the park and to other dog-friendly places where he will encounter new people, especially children. Puppies automatically recognize children as "little

people" and are drawn to play with them. Just make sure that you supervise these meetings and that the children do not get too rough or encourage him to play too hard. Likewise, an overzealous pup can often nip too hard, frightening the child and in turn making the puppy overly excited. A bad experience in puppyhood can impact a dog for life, so a pup that has a negative experience with a child may grow up to be shy or even aggressive around children.

THE FIRST FAMILY MEETING
Your puppy's first day at home should be quiet and uneventful. As active as puppies are, they need plenty of time to rest, too. Let him make friends with other members of the family on his own terms; don't overwhelm him. You have a lifetime ahead to get to know each other!

during this time should be gentle and positive. A frightening or negative event could leave a permanent impression that could affect his future behavior if a similar situation arises.

Also make sure that your puppy has received his first and second rounds of vaccinations before you expose him to other dogs or bring him to places that other dogs may frequent. Avoid dog parks and other strange-dog areas until your vet assures you that your puppy is fully immunized and resistant to the

As your Basenji grows up, you will eventually switch him to an adult dog food. Your breeder or vet can offer advice about food choices for the Basenji.

Take your puppy along on your daily errands. Puppies are natural "people magnets," and most people who see your pup will want to pet him. Don't force things and don't let the pup become overwhelmed, and these encounters will help to mold him into a confident adult dog.

Be cautious when introducing your Basenji pup to other dogs, as the breed does not particularly like being approached by strange dogs. Though the Basenji is not usually dog-aggressive, be sensitive to your African baby's aloof and cautious nature. Never rush the proceedings; let the Basenji approach other dogs at his own pace.

Be especially careful of your puppy's encounters and experiences during the eight-to-ten-week-old period, which is also called the "fear period." This is a serious imprinting period, and all contact

diseases that can be passed between canines. Discuss safe early socialization with your breeder.

LEADER OF THE PUPPY'S PACK

Like other canines, your puppy needs an authority figure, someone he can look up to and regard as the leader of his "pack." His first pack leader was his dam, who taught him to be polite and not chew too hard on her ears or nip at her muzzle. He learned those same lessons from his littermates. If he played too rough, they cried in pain and stopped the game, which sent an important message to the rowdy puppy.

As puppies play together, they are also struggling to determine who will be the boss. Being pack animals, dogs need someone to be in charge. If a litter of puppies remained together beyond puppyhood, one of the pups would emerge as the strongest one, the one who calls the shots.

Once your puppy leaves the pack, he will look intuitively for a new leader. If he does not

Introductions to other dogs must be done with care to foster a good canine friendship. These two look like they're off on the right paw!

recognize you as that leader, he will try to assume that position for himself. Of course, it is hard to imagine your adorable Basenji puppy trying to be in charge when he is so small and seemingly helpless, but don't be fooled! The Basenji is an "alpha" breed, and these are natural canine instincts. Do not cave in and allow your pup to get the upper "paw"!

Just as socialization is so important during these first 20 weeks, so too is your puppy's early education. He was born without any bad habits. He does not know what is good or bad behavior. If he does things like nipping and digging, it's because he is having fun and doesn't know that humans consider these things as "bad." It's your job to teach him proper puppy manners, and this is the best time to accomplish that...before he has developed bad habits, since it

TASTY LESSONS

The best route to teaching a very young puppy is through his tummy. Use tiny bits of soft puppy treats to teach obedience commands like come, sit and down. Don't overdo treats: schooltime is not meant to be mealtime.

A sturdy leash and properly fitting collar are two essentials in your Basenji's training and safety. The leash must be securely attached to the collar.

is much more difficult to "unlearn" or correct unacceptable learned behavior than to teach good behavior from the start.

Make sure that all members of the family understand the importance of being consistent when training their new puppy. If you tell the puppy to stay off the sofa and your daughter allows him to cuddle on the couch with her to watch her favorite TV show, your pup will be confused about what he is and is not allowed to do. Have a family conference before your pup comes home so that everyone understands the basic principles of puppy training and the rules you have set forth for the pup, and agrees to follow them.

The old saying that "an ounce of prevention is worth a pound of cure" is especially true when it comes to puppies. It is much easier to prevent inappropriate behavior than it is to change it. It's also easier and less stressful for the pup, since it will keep discipline to a minimum and create a more positive learning environment for him, an environment in which the Basenji learns quickly. That, in turn, will also be easier on you.

Here are a few commonsense tips to keep your belongings safe and your puppy out of trouble:

• Keep your closet doors closed and your shoes, socks and other apparel off the floor so your puppy can't get at them.
• Keep a secure lid on the trash container or put the trash where your puppy can't dig into it. He can't damage what he can't reach!
• Supervise your puppy at all times to make sure he is not getting into mischief. If he starts to chew the corner of the rug, you can distract him instantly by tossing a toy for him to fetch. You also will be able to whisk him outside when you notice

WATCH THE WATER
To help your puppy sleep through the night without having to relieve himself, remove his water bowl after 7 p.m. Offer him a couple of ice cubes during the evening to quench his thirst. Never leave water in a puppy's crate, as this is inviting puddles of mishaps.

that he is about to piddle on the carpet. If you can't see your puppy, you can't teach him or correct his behavior.

SOLVING PUPPY PROBLEMS

CHEWING AND NIPPING
Nipping at fingers and toes is normal puppy behavior. Chewing is also the way that puppies investigate their surroundings. However, you will have to teach your puppy that chewing anything other than his toys is not acceptable. That won't happen overnight and at times puppy teeth will test your patience. However, if you allow nipping and inappropriate chewing to continue, just think about the damage that a mature Basenji can do with a full set of adult teeth.

Whenever your puppy nips your hand or fingers, cry out "Ouch!" in a loud voice, which should startle your puppy and stop him from nipping, even if only for a moment. Immediately distract him by offering a small treat or an appropriate toy for him to chew instead (which means having chew toys and puppy treats handy or in your pockets at all times). Praise him when he takes the toy and tell him what a good fellow he is. Praise is just as or even more important in puppy training as discipline and correction.

Puppies also tend to nip at children more often than adults, since they perceive little ones to be more vulnerable and more similar to their littermates. Teach your children appropriate responses to nipping behavior. If they are unable to handle it themselves, you may have to intervene. Puppy nips can be quite painful and a child's frightened reaction will only encourage a puppy to nip harder, which is a natural canine response. As with all other puppy situations, interaction between your Basenji puppy and children should be supervised.

Chewing on objects, not just family members' fingers and ankles,

Basenjis are best taught with a consistent method based on positive reinforcement.

To a pup, nothing is off limits when it comes to chewing!

is also normal canine behavior that can be especially tedious (for the owner, not the pup) during the teething period when the puppy's adult teeth are coming in. At this stage, chewing just plain feels good. Furniture legs and cabinet corners are common puppy favorites. Shoes and other personal items also taste pretty good to a pup.

The best solution is, once again, prevention. If you value something, keep it tucked away and out of reach. You can't hide your dining-room table in a closet, but you can try to deflect the chewing by applying a bitter product made just to deter dogs from chewing. Available in a spray or cream, this substance is vile-tasting, although safe for dogs, and most puppies will avoid the forbidden object after one tiny taste. You also can apply the product to your leather leash if the puppy tries to chew on his lead during leash-training sessions.

Keep a ready supply of safe chews handy to offer your Basenji as a distraction when he starts to chew on something that's a "no-

no." Remember, at this tender age he does not yet know what is permitted or forbidden, so you have to be "on call" every minute he's awake and on the prowl. Your guidance will help him develop lifelong proper chewing habits.

You may lose a treasure or two during puppy's growing-up period, and the furniture could sustain a nasty nick or two. These can be trying times, so be prepared for those inevitable accidents and comfort yourself in knowing that this too shall pass.

PUPPY WHINING

Puppies often cry and whine, just as infants and little children do. It's their way of telling us that they are lonely or in need of attention. Your puppy will miss his littermates and will feel insecure when he is left alone. You may be out of the house or just in another room, but he will still feel alone. During these times, the puppy's crate should be his personal comfort station, a place all his own where he can feel safe and secure. Once he learns that being alone is okay and not something to be feared, he will settle down without crying or objecting. You might want to leave a radio on while he is crated, as the sound of human voices can be soothing and will give the impression that people are around.

Give your puppy a favorite cuddly toy or chew toy to entertain him whenever he is crated. You will both be happier: the puppy because he is safe in his den and you because he is quiet, safe and not getting into puppy escapades that can wreak havoc in your house or cause him danger.

To make sure that your puppy will always view his crate as a safe and cozy place, never, ever, use the crate as punishment. That's the best way to turn the crate into a negative place that the pup will want to avoid. Sure, you can use the crate for your own peace of mind if your puppy is getting into trouble and needs some "time out." Just don't let him know that! Never scold the pup and immediately place him into the crate. Count to ten, give him a couple of hugs and maybe a treat, then scoot him into his crate.

It's also important not to make a big fuss when he is released from the crate. That will make getting out of the crate more appealing than being in the crate, which is just the opposite of what you are trying to achieve.

FOOD GUARDING

Some dogs are picky eaters; others seem to inhale their food without chewing it. Occasionally the true "chow hound" will become protective of his food, which is one dangerous step toward other aggressive behavior. Food guarding is obvious: your puppy will growl, snarl or even attempt to bite you if you approach his

---

GETTING ACQUAINTED

When visiting a litter, ask the breeder for suggestions on how best to interact with the puppies. If possible, get right into the middle of the pack and sit down with them. Observe which pups climb into your lap and which ones shy away. Toss a toy for them to chase and bring back to you. It's easy to fall in love with the puppy who picks you, but keep your future objectives in mind before you make your final decision.

---

food bowl or put your hand into his pan while he's eating.

This behavior is not acceptable, and very preventable! If your puppy is an especially voracious eater, sit next to him occasionally while he eats and dangle your fingers in his food bowl. Don't feed him in a corner, where he could feel possessive of his eating space. Rather, place his food bowl in an open area of your kitchen where you are in close proximity. Occasionally remove his food in mid-meal, tell him he's a good boy and return his bowl.

If your pup becomes possessive of his food, look for other signs of future aggression, like guarding his favorite toys or refusing to obey obedience commands that he knows. Consult an obedience trainer for help in reinforcing obedience so your Basenji will fully understand that *you* are the boss.

BASENJI

Adding a Basenji to your household means adding a new family member who will need your care each and every day. When your Basenji pup first comes home, you will start a routine with him so that, as he grows up, your dog will have a daily schedule just as you do. The aspects of your dog's daily care will likewise become regular parts of your day, so you'll both have a new schedule. Dogs learn by consistency and thrive on routine: regular times for meals, exercise, grooming and potty trips are just as important for your dog as they are to you. Your dog's schedule will depend much on your family's daily routine, but remember that you now have a new member of the family who is part of your day every day.

FEEDING

Feeding your dog the best diet is based on various factors, including age, activity level, overall condition, health and size. When you visit the breeder, he will share with you his advice about the proper diet for your dog based on his experience with the breed and the foods with which he has had success. Likewise, your vet will be a helpful source of advice throughout the dog's life and will aid you in planning a diet for optimal health.

FEEDING THE PUPPY

Of course, your pup's very first food will be his dam's milk. There may be special situations in which pups fail to nurse, necessitating that the breeder hand-feed them with a formula, but for the most part pups spend the first weeks of life nursing from their dam. The breeder weans the pups by gradually introducing solid foods and decreasing the milk meals. Pups may even start themselves off on the weaning process, albeit inadvertently, if they snatch bites from their mom's food bowl.

By the time the pups are ready for new homes, they are fully weaned and eating a good puppy food. As a new owner, you may be thinking, "Great! The breeder has taken care of the hard part." Not so fast.

Basenji puppies, like other puppies, instinctively want to nurse from their mother. Mother's milk supplies colostrum, a sort of antibiotic, which protects the puppy during his first weeks of life.

A puppy's first year of life is the time when all or most of his growth and development takes place. This is a delicate time, and diet plays a huge role in proper skeletal and muscular formation. Improper diet and exercise habits can lead to damaging problems that will compromise the dog's health and movement for his entire life. That being said, new owners should not worry needlessly. With the myriad types of food formulated specifically for growing pups of different-sized breeds, dog-food manufacturers have taken much of the guesswork out of feeding your puppy well. Since growth-food formulas are

FREE FEEDING

Many owners opt to feed their dogs the free way. That is, they serve dry kibble in a feeder that is available to the dog all day. Arguably, this is the most convenient method of feeding an adult dog, but it may encourage the dog to become fussy about food or defensive over his bowl and it does not allow the owner to accurately gauge how much his dog is eating.

designed to provide the nutrition that a growing puppy needs, it is unnecessary and, in fact, can prove harmful to add supplements to the diet. Research has shown that too much of certain vitamin supplements and minerals predispose a dog to skeletal problems. It's by no means a case of "if a little is good, a lot is better." At every stage of your dog's life, too much or too little in the way of nutrients can be harmful, which is why a manufactured complete food is the easiest way to know that your dog is getting what he needs.

Because of a young pup's small body and accordingly small digestive system, his daily portion will be divided up into small meals throughout the day. This can mean starting off with three or more meals a day and decreasing the number of meals as the pup matures. It is generally thought

Puppyhood is a crucial feeding time, as the pup needs good nutrition for healthy growth.

> ## SWITCHING FOODS
>
> There are certain times in a dog's life when it becomes necessary to switch his food; for example, from puppy to adult food and then from adult to senior-dog food. Additionally, you may decide to feed your pup a different type of food from what he received from the breeder, and there may be "emergency" situations in which you can't find your dog's normal brand and have to offer something else temporarily. Anytime a change is made, for whatever reason, the switch must be done gradually. You don't want to upset the dog's stomach or end up with a picky eater who refuses to eat something new. A tried-and-true approach is, over the course of about a week, to mix a little of the new food in with the old, increasing the proportion of new to old as the days progress. At the end of the week, you'll be feeding his regular portions of the new food, and he will barely notice the change.

that dividing the day's food into two meals on a morning/evening schedule is healthier for the dog's digestion, allowing adequate time for the dog to rest before and after mealtimes before he is allowed to exercise.

Regarding the feeding schedule, feeding the pup at the same times and in the same place each day is important for both housebreaking purposes and establishing the dog's everyday routine. As for the amount to feed, growing puppies generally need proportionately more food per body weight than their adult counterparts, but a pup should never be allowed to gain excess weight. Dogs of all ages should be kept in proper body condition, but extra weight can strain a pup's developing frame, causing skeletal problems.

Watch your pup's weight as he grows and, if the recommended amounts seem to be too much or too little for your pup, consult the vet about appropriate dietary changes. Keep in mind that treats, although small, can quickly add up throughout the day, contributing unnecessary calories. Treats are fine when used prudently; opt for dog treats specially formulated to be healthy or for nutritious snacks like small pieces of cheese or cooked chicken. Be careful about offering "people food" treats, as certain foods, such as chocolate, onions, grapes, raisins and nuts, are known to be toxic to dogs.

FEEDING THE ADULT DOG

For the adult (meaning physically mature) dog, feeding properly is about maintenance, not growth. Again, correct weight is a concern. Your dog should appear fit and should have an evident "waist." His ribs should not be protruding (a sign of being

DIET DON'TS

- Got milk? Don't give it to your dog! Dogs cannot tolerate large quantities of cows' milk, as they do not have the enzymes to digest lactose.
- You may have heard of dog owners who add raw eggs to their dogs' food for a shiny coat or to make the food more palatable, but consumption of raw eggs too often can cause a deficiency of the vitamin biotin.
- Avoid feeding table scraps, as they will upset the balance of the dog's complete food. Additionally, fatty or highly seasoned foods can cause upset canine stomachs.
- Do not offer raw meat to your dog. Raw meat can contain parasites; it also is high in fat.
- Vitamin A toxicity in dogs can be caused by too much raw liver, especially if the dog already gets enough vitamin A in his balanced diet, which should be the case.
- Bones like chicken, pork chop and other soft bones are not suitable, as they easily splinter.

underweight), but they should be covered by only a slight layer of fat. An extra pound or two, as well as a too-thin frame, will be easy to notice on a Basenji. Under normal circumstances, an adult dog can be maintained fairly easily with a high-quality nutritionally complete adult-formula food.

Factor treats into your dog's overall daily caloric intake and avoid offering table scraps. Overweight dogs are more prone to health problems. Research has even shown that obesity takes years off a dog's life. With that in mind, resist the urge to overfeed and over-treat. Don't make unnecessary additions to your dog's diet, whether with tidbits or with extra vitamins and minerals.

The amount of food needed for proper maintenance will vary depending on the individual dog's activity level, but you will be able to tell whether the daily portions

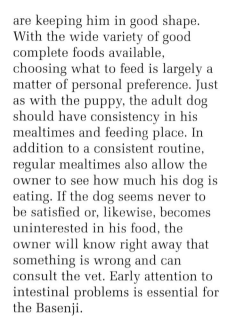

are keeping him in good shape. With the wide variety of good complete foods available, choosing what to feed is largely a matter of personal preference. Just as with the puppy, the adult dog should have consistency in his mealtimes and feeding place. In addition to a consistent routine, regular mealtimes also allow the owner to see how much his dog is eating. If the dog seems never to be satisfied or, likewise, becomes uninterested in his food, the owner will know right away that something is wrong and can consult the vet. Early attention to intestinal problems is essential for the Basenji.

DIETS FOR THE AGING DOG

A good rule of thumb is that once a dog has reached 75% of his expected lifespan, he has reached "senior citizen" or geriatric status. Your Basenji will be considered a senior at about 9 years of age; he has an average projected lifespan of 12–14 years, though many live longer, some even 16–17 years.

What does aging have to do with your dog's diet? No, he won't get a discount at the local diner's early-bird special. Yes, he will require some dietary changes to accommodate the changes that come along with increased age. One change is that the older dog's dietary needs become more similar to that of a puppy. Specifically, dogs can metabolize

---

HOLD THE ONIONS

Sliced, chopped or grated; dehydrated, boiled, fried or raw; pearl, Spanish, white or red: onions can be deadly to your dog. The toxic effects of onions in dogs are cumulative for up to 30 days. A serious form of anemia, called Heinz body anemia, affects the red blood cells of dogs that have eaten onions. For safety (and better breath), dogs should avoid chives and scallions as well.

more protein as youngsters and seniors than in the adult-maintenance stage. Discuss with your vet whether you need to switch to a higher-protein or senior-formulated food or whether your current adult-dog food contains sufficient nutrition for the senior.

Watching the dog's weight remains essential, even more so in the senior stage. Older dogs are already more vulnerable to illness, and obesity only contributes to their susceptibility to problems. As the older dog becomes less active and, thus, exercises less, his regular portions may cause him to gain weight. At this point,

NOT HUNGRY?

No dog in his right mind would turn down his dinner, would he? If you notice that your dog has lost interest in his food, there could be any number of causes. Basenjis can be affected by certain intestinal problems, and dental problems are also common causes of appetite loss, one that is often overlooked. If your dog has a toothache, a loose tooth or sore gums from infection, chances are it doesn't feel so good to chew. Think about when you've had a toothache! If your dog does not approach the food bowl with his usual enthusiasm, look inside his mouth for signs of a problem. Whatever the cause, you'll want to consult your vet so that your chow hound can get back to his happy, hungry self as soon as possible.

you may consider decreasing his daily food intake or switching to a reduced-calorie food. As with other changes, you should consult your vet for advice.

TYPES OF FOOD AND READING THE LABEL

When selecting the type of food to feed your dog, it is important to check out the label for ingredients. Many dry-food products have soybean, corn or rice as the main ingredient. The main ingredient will be listed first on the label, with the rest of the ingredients following in descending order according to their proportion in the food. While these types of dry food are fine, you should look into dry foods based on meat or fish. These are better-quality foods and thus higher priced. However, they may be just as economical in the long run, because studies have shown that it takes less of the higher-

When offering food and water to a puppy, spill-proof is important!

quality foods to maintain a dog.

Comparing the various types of food, dry, canned and semi-moist, dry foods contain the least amount of water and canned foods the most. Proportionately, dry foods are the most calorie- and nutrient-dense, which means that you need more of a canned food product to supply the same amount of nutrition. In households with breeds of disparate size, the canned/dry/semi-moist question can be of special importance. Larger breeds obviously eat more than smaller ones and thus in general do better on dry foods, but smaller breeds do fine on canned foods and require "small bite" formulations to protect their small mouths and teeth if fed only dry foods. You may find success mixing the food types as well. Some Basenji breeders advocate natural diets as a way of protecting from or treating certain medical problems, but an owner must be thoroughly educated in this before attempting to create a proper diet on his own. Water is important for all dogs, but even more so for those fed dry foods, as there is no water content in their food.

There are strict controls that regulate the nutritional content of dog food, and a food has to meet the minimum requirements in order to be considered "complete and balanced." It is important that you choose such a food for your dog, so check the label to be sure that your chosen food meets the requirements. If not, look for a food that clearly states on the label that it is formulated to be complete and balanced for your dog's particular stage of life.

Recommendations for amounts to feed will also be indicated on the label. You should also ask your vet about proper food portions, and you will keep an eye on your dog's condition to see whether the recommended amounts are adequate. If he becomes over- or underweight, you will need to make adjustments; this also would be a good

---

QUENCHING HIS THIRST

Is your dog drinking more than normal and trying to lap up everything in sight? Excessive drinking has many different causes. Obvious causes for a dog's being thirstier than usual are hot weather and vigorous exercise. However, if your dog is drinking more for no apparent reason, you could have cause for concern. Serious conditions like Fanconi syndrome, kidney or liver disease, diabetes and various types of hormonal problems can all be indicated by excessive drinking. If you notice your dog's being excessively thirsty, contact your vet at once. Hopefully there will be a simpler explanation, but the earlier a serious problem is detected, the sooner it can be treated, with a better rate of cure.

FEEDING IN HOT WEATHER

Even the most dedicated chow hound may have less of an appetite when the weather is hot or humid. If your dog leaves more of his food behind than usual, adjust his portions until the weather and his appetite return to normal. Never leave the uneaten portion in the bowl, hoping he will return to finish it, because higher temperatures encourage food spoilage and bacterial growth.

time to consult your vet.

The food label may also make feeding suggestions, such as whether moistening a dry-food product is recommended. Sometimes a splash of water will make the food more palatable for the dog and even enhance the flavor; it will also prevent a "chow hound" from inhaling his food and thus upsetting his stomach. Don't be overwhelmed by the many factors that go into feeding your dog. Manufacturers of complete and balanced foods make it easy, and once you find the right food and amounts for your Basenji, his daily feeding will be a matter of routine.

DON'T FORGET THE WATER!

For a dog, it's always time for a drink! Regardless of what type of food he eats, there's no doubt that he needs plenty of water. Fresh cold water, in a clean bowl, should be freely available to your dog at all times. There are special circumstances, such as during puppy housebreaking, when you will want to monitor your pup's water intake so that you will be able to predict when he will need to relieve himself, but water must be available to him nonetheless. Water is essential for hydration and proper body function just as it is in humans.

You will get to know how much your dog typically drinks in a day. Of course, in the heat or if exercising, he will be more thirsty and will drink more. However, if he begins to drink noticeably more water for no apparent reason, this could signal any of various problems, and you are advised to consult your vet.

Water is the best drink for dogs. Some owners are tempted to give milk from time to time or to

Ever alert and ready to go, this hunter cannot be trusted off leash. Consider your Basenji's safety when providing him with opportunities to exercise.

moisten dry food with milk, but dogs do not have the enzymes necessary to digest the lactose in milk, which is much different from the milk that nursing puppies receive. Therefore, stick with clean fresh water to quench your dog's thirst, and always have it readily available to him.

EXERCISE

The Basenji is an active breed, so exercise is necessary for a Basenji's health and happiness. How a Basenji is best exercised depends very much on the area in which you live, but if possible a lead walk with an opportunity for a good free run should be a daily routine.

Free runs should, of course, only be allowed in places that are completely safe,

PUPPY STEPS

Puppies are brimming with activity and enthusiasm. It seems that they can play all day and night without tiring, but don't overdo your puppy's exercise regimen. Easy does it for the puppy's first six to nine months. Keep walks brief and don't let the puppy engage in stressful jumping games. The puppy frame is delicate, and too much exercise during those critical growing months can cause injury to his bone structure, ligaments and musculature. Save his first jog for his first birthday!

so all possible escape routes should be thoroughly investigated before letting a dog off the lead. After exercise he should be allowed to settle down quietly for a little rest, and not fed for a full hour.

Because Basenjis are escapologists, it goes without saying that garden and run areas must be completely dog-proof—or "Basenji-proof" would probably be a better description! As Basenjis are usually capable of climbing chain-link fencing, some owners like to have this only loosely strung, so that dogs do not consider it sufficiently secure to climb. Hedges grown alongside a fence act as an additional deterrent.

GROOMING

Basenjis need little grooming and are virtually free from doggy odors. Added to this, they enjoy grooming themselves, so if one has a Basenji around the home, he's usually a permanently clean house companion.

Even when showing a Basenji, little grooming is required; indeed, some people prefer not to do any at all. However, most people like to give the coat a brush, then go over the coat with a hound glove to add the finishing touches. Hound gloves do vary, but a useful one is chamois leather on one side and velvet on the other. A good wipe-over with

A hound glove gives the Basenji's coat a nice sheen. INSET: A fine-toothed comb can be used to detect and remove fleas on the Basenji.

the chamois side, and then the velvet one, produces a nice sheen on the coat and provides good stimulation for the skin.

BATHING

In general, dogs need to be bathed only a few times a year, possibly more often if your dog gets into something messy or if he starts to smell like a dog. Show dogs are usually bathed before every show, which could be as frequent as weekly, although this depends on the owner. Bathing too frequently can have negative effects on the skin and coat, removing natural oils and causing dryness. Bathing is only needed occasionally, but always remember that Basenjis have sensitive skin, so mild

shampoos and conditioners are the most suitable. If ever a product used on the coat causes the skin to become raw, stop using it immediately.

If you give your dog his first bath when he is young, he will become accustomed to the process. Wrestling a dog into the tub or chasing a freshly shampooed dog who has escaped from the bath will be no fun! Most dogs don't naturally enjoy their baths, but you at least want yours to cooperate with you.

Before bathing the dog, have the items you'll need close at hand. First, decide where you will bathe the dog. You should have a tub or basin with a non-slip surface. Puppies can even be bathed in a sink. In warm weather, some like to use a portable pool in the yard, although you'll want to make sure your dog doesn't head for the nearest dirt pile following his bath! You will also need a hose or shower spray to wet the coat thoroughly, a shampoo formulated for dogs and some absorbent towels. Human shampoos are too harsh for dogs' coats and will dry them out.

Before wetting the dog, give him a brush-through to remove any dead hair, dirt and mats. Make sure he is at ease in the tub and have the water at a comfortable temperature. Begin bathing by wetting the coat all the way

WATER SHORTAGE

No matter how well behaved your dog is, bathing is always a project especially with the water-hating Basenji! Nothing can substitute for a good warm bath, but owners do have the option of giving their dogs "dry" baths. Pet shops sell excellent products, in both powder and spray forms, designed for spot-cleaning your dog. These dry shampoos are convenient for touch-up jobs when you don't have the time to bathe your dog in the traditional way.

Muddy feet, messy behinds and smelly coats can be spot-cleaned and deodorized with a "wet-nap"-style cleaner. On those days when your dog insists on rolling in fresh goose droppings and there's no time for a bath, a spot bath can save the day. These pre-moistened wipes are also handy for other grooming needs like wiping faces, ears and eyes and freshening tails and behinds.

NAIL CLIPPING

Having his nails trimmed is not on many dogs' lists of favorite things to do. With this in mind, you will need to accustom your puppy to the procedure at a young age so that he will sit still (well, as still as he can) for his pedicures. Long nails can cause the dog's feet to spread, which is not good for him; likewise, long nails can hurt if they unintentionally scratch, not good for you! The toenails should be kept short, especially on a Basenji, as this will help to keep the toes neat and arched.

Some dogs' nails are worn down naturally by regular walking on hard surfaces, so the frequency

Most of the moisture can be removed from the coat by drying with an absorbent towel.

down to the skin. Massage in the shampoo, keeping it away from his face and eyes. Rinse him thoroughly, again avoiding the eyes and ears, as you don't want to get water into the ear canals. A thorough rinsing is important, as shampoo residue is drying and itchy to the dog. After rinsing, wrap him in a towel to absorb the initial moisture. You can finish drying with a fresh dry towel. You should keep the dog indoors and away from drafts until he is completely dry.

with which you clip depends on your individual dog. Look at his nails from time to time and clip as needed; a good way to know when it's time for a trim is if you hear your dog clicking as he walks across the floor.

There are several types of nail clippers and even electric nail-grinding tools made for dogs; first we'll discuss using the clipper. To start, have your clipper ready and some doggie treats on hand. You want your pup to view his nail-clipping sessions in a positive light, and what better way to

In between grooming sessions, check your Basenji's coat and skin to make sure he hasn't picked up anything (insect bites, rashes, allergies) from time spent outdoors.

convince him than with food? You may want to enlist the help of an assistant to comfort the pup and offer treats as you concentrate on the clipping itself. The guillotine-type clipper is thought of by many as the easiest type to use; the nail tip is inserted into the opening, and blades on the top and bottom snip it off in one clip.

Start by grasping the pup's paw; a little pressure on the foot pad causes the nail to extend, making it easier to clip. Clip off a little at a time. If you can see the "quick," which is a blood vessel that runs through each nail, you will know how much to trim, as you do not want to cut into the quick. On that note, if you do cut the quick, which will cause bleeding, you can stem the flow of blood with a styptic pencil or other clotting agent. If you mistakenly nip the quick, do not panic or fuss, as this will cause the pup to be afraid. Simply reassure the pup, stop the bleeding and move on to the next nail. Don't be discouraged; you will become a professional canine pedicurist with practice.

You may or may not be able to see the quick, so it's best to just clip off a small bit at a time. If you see a dark dot in the center of the nail, this is the quick and your cue to stop clipping. Tell the puppy he's a "good boy" and offer a piece of treat with each nail. You can also use nail-clipping

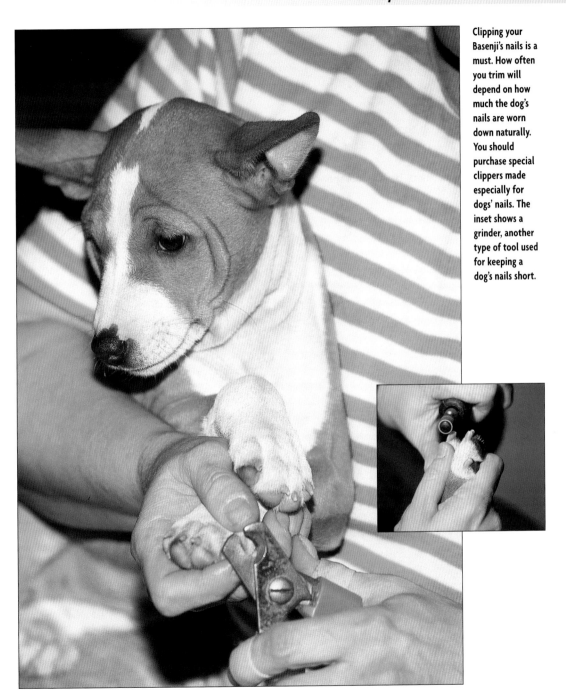

Clipping your Basenji's nails is a must. How often you trim will depend on how much the dog's nails are worn down naturally. You should purchase special clippers made especially for dogs' nails. The inset shows a grinder, another type of tool used for keeping a dog's nails short.

time to examine the footpads, making sure that they are not dry and cracked and that nothing has become embedded in them.

The nail grinder, the other choice, is many owners' first choice. Accustoming the puppy to the sound of the grinder and sensation of the buzz presents fewer challenges than the clipper, and there's no chance of cutting through the quick. Use the grinder on a low setting and always talk soothingly to your dog. He won't mind his salon visit, and he'll have nicely polished nails as well.

EAR CLEANING

While keeping your dog's ears clean unfortunately will not cause him to "hear" your commands any better, it will protect him from ear infection and ear-mite

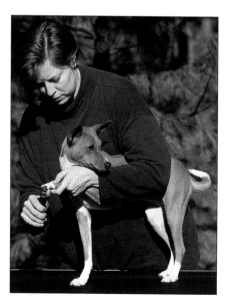

Show groomers use a grooming table to make grooming tasks easier; pet owners may want to consider this as well.

infestation. In addition, a dog's ears are vulnerable to waxy build-up and to collecting foreign matter from the outdoors. Look in your dog's ears regularly to ensure that they look pink, clean and otherwise healthy. Even if they look fine, an odor in the ears signals a problem and means it's time to call the vet.

A dog's ears should be cleaned regularly; once a week is suggested, and you can do this along with your regular brushing. Using a cotton ball or pad and never probing into the ear canal, wipe the ear gently. You can use an ear-cleansing liquid or powder available from your vet or pet-supply store; alternatively, you might prefer to use home-made solutions with ingredients like one part white vinegar and one part hydrogen peroxide. Ask your vet about home remedies before you attempt to concoct something on your own!

Keep your dog's ears free of excess hair by plucking it as needed. If done gently, this will be painless for the dog. Look for wax, brown droppings (a sign of ear mites), redness or any other abnormalities. At the first sign of a problem, contact your vet so that he can prescribe an appropriate medication.

EYE CARE

During grooming sessions, pay extra attention to the condition of your dog's eyes. If the area around the eyes is soiled or if tear staining has occurred, there are various cleaning agents made especially for this purpose. Look at the dog's eyes to make sure no debris has entered; dogs with large eyes and those who spend time outdoors are especially prone to this.

The signs of an eye infection are obvious: mucus, redness, puffiness, scabs or other signs of irritation. If your dog's eyes become infected, the vet will likely prescribe an antibiotic ointment for treatment. If you notice signs of more serious problems, such as opacities in the eye, which usually indicate cataracts, consult the vet at once. Taking time to pay attention to your dog's eyes will alert you in the early stages of any problem so that you can get your dog treatment as soon as possible. You could save your dog's sight!

A CLEAN SMILE

Another essential part of grooming is brushing your dog's teeth and checking his overall oral condition. Studies show that around 80% of dogs experience dental problems by two years of age, and the percentage is higher in older dogs. Therefore it is highly likely that your dog will have trouble with his teeth and gums unless you are proactive with home dental care.

Your Basenji's ears require regular attention to keep them free of dirt, mites and other irritants. Ear cleaning drops, along with a soft cotton pad, will help keep your dog's ears clean.

The most common dental problem in dogs is plaque build-up. If not treated, this causes gum disease, infection and resultant tooth loss. Bacteria from these infections spread throughout the body, affecting the vital organs. Do you need much more convincing to start brushing your dog's teeth? If so, take a good whiff of your dog's breath, and read on.

Fortunately, home dental care is rather easy and convenient for pet owners. Specially formulated canine toothpaste is easy to find. You should use one of these toothpastes, not a product for humans. Some doggie pastes are even available in flavors appealing to dogs. If your dog likes the flavor, he will tolerate the process better, making things much easier for you! Doggie toothbrushes come in different sizes and are designed to fit the contour of a canine mouth. Rubber fingertip

UNIQUE BASENJI TRAITS

Basenjis don't drink a great deal of water. This is another of their cat-like traits, for cats don't drink much water. Another useful thing to know is that a Basenji's average temperature is one degree lower than that of other dogs. When visiting the vet, it is wise to mention this.

As a native African breed, Basenjis are used to living in a warm climate. Consequently, they do feel the cold, so canine coats, readily available from dog shows and good pet stores, can be useful on outdoor trips during the winter months. Obviously, when out hunting and running free, their body temperature rises naturally.

brushes fit right on one of your fingers and have rubber nodes to clean the teeth and massage the gums. This may be easier to handle, as it is akin to rubbing your dog's teeth with your finger.

As with other grooming tasks, accustom your Basenji pup to his dental care early on. Start gently, for a few minutes at a time, so that he gets used to the feel of the brush and to your handling his mouth. Offer praise and petting so that he looks at tooth-care time as a time when he gets extra love and attention. The routine should become second nature; he may not like it, but he should at least tolerate it.

Aside from brushing, offer dental toys to your dog and feed crunchy biscuits, which help to minimize plaque. Rope toys have the added benefit of acting like floss as the dog chews. At your adult dog's yearly check-ups, the vet will likely perform a thorough tooth scraping as well as a complete check for any problems. Proper care of your dog's teeth will ensure that you will enjoy your dog's smile for many years to come. The next time your dog goes to give you a hello kiss, you'll be glad you spent the time caring for his teeth.

THE OTHER END

Dogs sometime have troubles with their anal glands, which are sacs located beside the anal vent. These should empty when a dog has normal bowel movements; if they don't, they can become full or impacted, causing discomfort. Owners often are alarmed to see their dogs scooting across the floor, dragging their behinds behind, this is just a dog's attempt to empty the glands himself.

Some brave owners attempt to evacuate their dogs' anal glands themselves during grooming, but no one will tell you that this is a pleasant task! Thus, many owners prefer to make the trip to the vet to have the vet take care of the problem; owners whose dogs visit a groomer can have this done by the groomer if he offers this as part of his services. Regardless, don't neglect the dog's other end in your home-care routine. Look for scooting, licking or other signs of discomfort "back there" to ascertain whether the anal glands need to be emptied.

IDENTIFICATION AND TRAVEL

ID FOR YOUR DOG

You love your Basenji and want to keep him safe. Of course you take every precaution to prevent his escaping from the yard or becoming lost or stolen. You have a sturdy high fence and you always keep your dog on lead when out and about in public places. If your dog is not properly identified, however, you are overlooking a major aspect of his safety. We hope to never be in a

A Basenji without ID is a lost dog waiting to happen. Consider the breed's "escapology" talents—need we say more?

situation where our dog is missing, but we should practice prevention in the unfortunate case that this happens; identification greatly increases the chances of your dog's being returned to you.

There are several ways to identify your dog. First, the traditional dog tag should be a staple in your dog's wardrobe, attached to his everyday collar. Tags can be made of sturdy plastic and various metals and should include your contact information so that a person who finds the dog can get in touch with you right away to arrange his return. Many people today enjoy the wide range of decorative tags available, so have fun and create a tag to match your dog's personality. Of course, it is important that the tag stays on the collar, so have a secure "O" ring attachment; you also can explore the type of tag that slides right onto the collar.

> **DOGGONE!**
> Wendy Ballard is the editor and publisher of the *DogGone*™ newsletter, which comes out bi-monthly and features fun articles by dog owners who love to travel with their dogs. The newsletter includes information about fun places to go with your dog, including popular vacation spots, dog-friendly hotels, parks, campgrounds, resorts, etc., as well as interesting activities to do with your dog, such as flyball, agility and much more. You can subscribe to the publication by contacting the publisher at PO Box 651155, Vero Beach, FL 32965-1155.

ID tags, which should indicate the dog's name and the owner's contact information, should be securely attached to the dog's collar and worn at all times.

In addition to the ID tag, which every dog should wear even if identified by another method, two other forms of identification have become popular: microchipping and tattooing. In microchipping, a tiny scannable chip is painlessly inserted under the dog's skin. The number is registered to you so that, if your lost dog turns up at a clinic or shelter, the chip can be scanned to retrieve your contact information.

The advantage of the microchip is that it is a permanent form of ID, but there are some factors to consider. Several different companies make microchips, and not all are compatible with the others' scanning devices. It's best to find a company with a universal microchip that can be read by scanners made by other companies as well. It won't do any good to have the dog chipped if the information cannot be retrieved. Also, not every humane society, shelter and clinic is equipped with a scanner, although more and more facilities are equipping themselves. In fact, many shelters microchip dogs that they adopt out to new homes.

Humane societies and veterinary clinics offer this service, which is usually very affordable. Because the microchip is not visible to the eye, the dog must wear a tag that states that he is microchipped so that whoever picks him up will know to have him scanned. He of course also should have a tag with contact information in case his chip cannot be read. Though less popular than microchipping, tattooing is another permanent method of ID for dogs. Most vets perform this service, and there are also clinics that perform dog tattooing. This is also an affordable procedure and one that will not cause much discomfort for the dog. It is best to put the tattoo in a visible area, such as the ear, to deter theft. It is sad to say that there are cases of dogs' being stolen and sold to research laboratories, but such laboratories will not accept tattooed dogs.

To ensure that the tattoo is effective in aiding your dog's return to you, the tattoo number must be registered with a national organization. That way, when someone finds a tattooed dog a phone call to the registry will quickly match the dog with his owner.

HIT THE ROAD

Car travel with your Basenji may be limited to necessity only, such as trips to the vet, or you may bring your dog along almost everywhere you go. This will depend much on your individual dog and how he reacts to rides in the car. You can begin desensitizing your dog to car travel as a pup so that it's something that he's used to. Still, some dogs suffer from motion sickness. Your vet may prescribe a medication for this if trips in the car pose a problem for your dog. At the very least, you will need to get him to the vet, so he will need to tolerate these trips with the least amount of hassle possible.

Start taking your pup on short trips, maybe just around the block to start. If he is fine with short trips, lengthen your rides a little at a time. Start to take him on your errands or just for drives around town. By this time it will be easy to tell whether your dog is a born traveler or would prefer staying at home when you are on the road.

Of course, safety is a concern for dogs in the car. First, he must travel securely, not left loose to roam about the car where he could be injured or distract the driver. A young pup can be held by a passenger initially but should soon graduate to a travel crate, which can be the same crate he uses in the home. Other options include a car harness (like a seat belt for dogs) and partitioning the back of the car with a gate made for this purpose.

Bring along what you will need for the dog. He should wear his collar and ID tags, of course, and you should bring his leash, water (and food if a long trip) and clean-up materials for potty breaks and in case of motion sickness. Always keep your dog on his leash when you make stops, and never leave him alone in the car. Many a dog has died from the heat inside a closed car; this does not take much time at all, even in cool weather. A dog left alone inside a car can also be a target for thieves.

PET OR STRAY?

Besides the obvious benefit of providing your contact information to whoever finds your lost dog, an ID tag makes your dog more approachable and more likely to be recovered. A strange dog wandering the neighborhood without a collar and tags will look like a stray, while the collar and tags indicate that the dog is someone's pet. Even if the ID tags become detached from the collar, the collar alone will make a person more likely to pick up the dog.

BASENJI

BE UPSTANDING!

You are the dog's leader. During training, stand up straight so your dog looks up at you, and therefore up *to* you. Say the command words distinctly, in a clear, declarative tone of voice. (No barking!) Give rewards only as the correct response takes place (remember your timing!). Praise, smiles and treats are "rewards" used to positively reinforce correct responses. Don't repeat a mistake. Just change to another exercise—you will soon find success.

BASIC TRAINING PRINCIPLES: PUPPY VS. ADULT

There's a big difference between training an adult dog and training a young puppy. With a young puppy, everything is new. At eight to ten weeks of age, he will be experiencing many things, and he has nothing with which to compare these experiences. Up to this point, he has been with his dam and littermates, not one-on-one with people except in his interactions with his breeder and visitors to the litter.

When you first bring the puppy home, he is eager to please you. This means that he accepts doing things your way. During the next couple of months, he will absorb the basis of everything he needs to know for the rest of his life. This early age is even referred to as the "sponge" stage. After that, for the next 18 months, it's up to you to reinforce good manners by building on the foundation that you've established. Once your puppy is reliable in basic commands and behavior and has reached the appropriate age, you may gradually introduce him to some of the interesting sports, games and activities available to pet owners and their dogs.

Raising your puppy is a family affair. Each member of the family must know what rules to set forth for the puppy and how to use the same one-word commands to mean exactly the same thing every time. Even if yours is a large family, one person will soon be considered by the pup to be the leader, the Alpha person in his pack, the "boss" who must be obeyed. Often that highly regarded person turns out to be the one who feeds the puppy. Food ranks very high on the puppy's list of important things! That's why your puppy is rewarded with small treats along with verbal praise when he responds to you correctly. As the puppy learns to do what you want him to do, the food rewards are gradually eliminated and

SHOULD WE ENROLL?

If you have the means and the time, you should definitely take your dog to obedience classes. Begin with Puppy Kindergarten classes in which puppies of all sizes learn basic lessons while getting the opportunity to meet and greet each other; it's as much about socialization as it is about good manners. What you learn in class you can practice at home. And if you goof up in practice, you'll get help in the next session.

only the praise remains. If you were to keep up with the food treats, you could have two problems on your hands—an obese dog and a beggar.

Training begins the minute your Basenji puppy steps through the doorway of your home, so don't make the mistake of putting the puppy on the floor and telling him by your actions to "Go for it! Run wild!" Even if this is your first puppy, you must act as if you know what you're doing: be the boss. An uncertain pup may be terrified to move, while a bold one will be ready to take you at your word and start

For those with show aspirations, training will progress from the basic commands to dog and handler learning ring procedure and how to work together for success.

You never know where you'll find your Basenji pup!

dog is trying to understand and learn your rules, at the same time he has to unlearn many of his previously self-taught habits and general view of the world.

Working with a professional trainer will speed up your progress with an adopted adult dog. You'll need patience, too. Some new rules may be close to impossible for the dog to accept. After all, he's been successful so far by doing everything his way! (Patience again.) He may agree with your instruction for a few days and then slip back into his old ways, so you must be just as consistent and understanding in your teaching as you would be with a puppy. (More patience needed yet again!) Your dog has to learn to pay attention to your

plotting to destroy the house (the latter more likely with a Basenji!) Before you collected your puppy, you decided where his own special place would be, and that's where to put him when you first arrive home. Give him a house tour after he has investigated his area and had a nap and a bathroom "pit stop."

It's worth mentioning here that, if you've adopted an adult dog that is completely trained to your liking, lucky you! You're off the hook! However, if that dog spent his life up to this point in a kennel, or even in a good home but without any real training, be prepared to tackle the job ahead. A dog three years of age or older with no previous training cannot be blamed for not knowing what he was never taught. While the

SMILE WHEN YOU ORDER ME AROUND!
While trainers recommend practicing with your dog every day, it's perfectly acceptable to take a "mental health day" off. It's better not to train the dog on days when you're in a sour mood. Your bad attitude or lack of interest will be sensed by your dog, and he will respond accordingly. Studies show that dogs are well tuned in to their humans' emotions. Be conscious of how you use your voice when talking to your dog. Raising your voice or shouting will only erode your dog's trust in you as his trainer and master.

voice, your family, the daily routine, new smells, new sounds and, in some cases, even a new climate.

One of the most important things to find out about a newly adopted adult dog is his reaction to children (yours and others), strangers and your friends, and how he acts upon meeting other dogs. If he was not socialized with dogs as a puppy, this could be a major problem. This does not mean that he's a "bad" dog, a vicious dog or an aggressive dog; rather, it means that he has no idea how to read another dog's body language. There's no way for him to tell whether the other dog is a friend or foe. Survival instinct takes over, telling him to attack first and ask questions later. This definitely calls for professional help and, even then, may not be a behavior that can be corrected 100% reliably (or even at all). This is why it is so very important to introduce any young puppy properly to other puppies and "dog-friendly" adult dogs; even more so with a Basenji, whose nature is aloof.

LEADER OF THE PACK

Canines are pack animals. They live according to pack rules, and every pack has only one leader. Guess what? That's you! To establish your position of authority, lay down the rules and be fair and good-natured in all your dealings with your dog. He will consider young children as his littermates, but the one who trains him, who feeds him, who grooms him, who expects him to come into line, that's his leader. And he who leads must be obeyed.

HOUSE-TRAINING YOUR BASENJI

Dogs are tactility-oriented when it comes to house-training. In other words, they respond to the surface on which they are given approval to eliminate. The choice is yours (the dog's version is in parentheses): the lawn (including the neighbors' lawns)? a bare patch of earth under a tree (where people like to sit and relax in the summertime)? concrete steps or patio (all sidewalks, garages and basement floors)? the curbside (watch out for cars)? a small area a city dog. Since Basenjis despise the rain, paper training proves advantageous for dog and owners.

WHEN YOUR PUPPY'S "GOT TO GO"
Your puppy's need to relieve himself is seemingly non-stop, but signs of improvement will be seen each week. From 8 to 10 weeks old, the puppy will have to be taken outside every time he wakes up, about 10–15 minutes after every meal and after every period of play—all day long, from first thing in the morning until his bedtime! That's a total of ten or more trips per day to teach the puppy where it's okay to relieve himself. With that schedule in mind, you can see that house-training a young puppy is not a part-time job. It requires someone to be home all day.

If that seems overwhelming or impossible, do a little planning. For example, plan to pick up your puppy at the start of a vacation period. If you can't get home in the middle of the day, plan to hire a dog-sitter or ask a neighbor to come over to take the pup outside, feed him his lunch and then take him out again about ten or so minutes after he's eaten. Also make arrangements with that or another person to be your "emergency" contact if you have to stay late on the job. Remind yourself—repeatedly—that this hectic schedule improves as the puppy gets older.

of crushed stone in a corner of the yard (mine!)? The latter is the best choice if you can manage it, because it will remain strictly for the dog's use and is easy to keep clean.

Basenjis are clean dogs, giving owners a distinct advantage in house-training. You can start out with paper-training indoors and switch over to an outdoor surface as the puppy matures and gains control over his need to eliminate. For the nay-sayers, don't worry—this won't mean that the dog will soil on every piece of newspaper lying around the house. You are training him to go outside, remember? Starting out by paper-training often is the only choice for

CANINE DEVELOPMENT SCHEDULE

It is important to understand how and at what age a puppy develops into adulthood. If you are a puppy owner, consult the following Canine Development Schedule to determine the stage of development your puppy is currently experiencing. This knowledge will help you as you work with the puppy in the weeks and months ahead.

PERIOD	AGE	CHARACTERISTICS
FIRST TO THIRD	BIRTH TO SEVEN WEEKS	Puppy needs food, sleep and warmth and responds to simple and gentle touching. Needs mother for security and disciplining. Needs littermates for learning and interacting with other dogs. Pup learns to function within a pack and learns pack order of dominance. Begin socializing pup with adults and children for short periods. Pup begins to become aware of his environment.
FOURTH	EIGHT TO TWELVE WEEKS	Brain is fully developed. Pup needs socializing with outside world. Remove from mother and littermates. Needs to change from canine pack to human pack. Human dominance necessary. Fear period occurs between 8 and 12 weeks. Avoid fright and pain.
FIFTH	THIRTEEN TO SIXTEEN WEEKS	Training and formal obedience should begin. Less association with other dogs, more with people, places, situations. Period will pass easily if you remember this is pup's change-to-adolescence time. Be firm and fair. Flight instinct prominent. Permissiveness and over-disciplining can do permanent damage. Praise for good behavior.
JUVENILE	FOUR TO EIGHT MONTHS	Another fear period about 7 to 8 months of age. It passes quickly, but be cautious of fright and pain. Sexual maturity reached. Dominant traits established. Dog should understand sit, down, come and stay by now.

NOTE: THESE ARE APPROXIMATE TIME FRAMES. ALLOW FOR INDIVIDUAL DIFFERENCES IN PUPPIES.

EXTRA! EXTRA!

The headlines read: "Puppy Piddles Here!" Breeders commonly use newspapers to line their whelping pens, so puppies learn to associate newspapers with relieving themselves. Do not use newspapers to line your pup's crate, as this will signal to your puppy that it is OK to urinate in his crate. If you choose to paper-train your puppy, you will layer newspapers on a section of the floor near the door he uses to go outside. You should encourage the puppy to use the papers to relieve himself, and bring him there whenever you see him getting ready to go. Little by little, you will reduce the size of the newspaper-covered area so that the puppy will learn to relieve himself "on the other side of the door."

HOME WITHIN A HOME

Your Basenji puppy needs to be confined to one secure, puppy-proof area when no one is able to watch his every move. Generally the kitchen is the place of choice because the floor is washable. Likewise, it's a busy family area that will accustom the pup to a variety of noises, everything from pots and pans to the telephone, blender and dishwasher. He will also be enchanted by the smell of your cooking (and will never be critical when you burn something). An exercise pen (also called an "ex-pen," a puppy version of a playpen) within the room of choice is an excellent

means of confinement for a young pup when you are there to supervise. He can see out and has a certain amount of space in which to run about, but he is safe from dangerous things like electrical cords, heating units, trash baskets or open kitchen-supply cabinets. Place the pen where the puppy will not get a blast of heat or air conditioning. When puppy is left alone, he should be put into his crate, as an unsupervised Basenji can climb out of an ex-pen easily.

In the pen, you can put a few toys, his bed (which can be his crate if the dimensions of pen and crate are compatible) and a

POTTY COMMAND

Most dogs love to please their masters; there are no bounds to what dogs will do to make their owners happy. The potty command is a good example of this theory. If toileting on command makes the master happy, then more power to him. Puppies will obligingly piddle if it really makes their keepers smile. Some owners can be creative about which word they will use to command their dogs to relieve themselves. Some popular choices are "Potty," "Tinkle," "Piddle," "Let's go," "Hurry up" and "Toilet." Give the command every time your puppy goes into position and the puppy will begin to associate his business with the command.

Once trained, your Basenji will reliably go to his chosen spot to relieve himself.

few layers of newspaper in one small corner, just in case. A water bowl can be hung at a convenient height on the side of the ex-pen so it won't become a splashing pool for an innovative puppy. His food dish can go on the floor, near but not under the water bowl.

Crates are something that pet owners are at last getting used to for their dogs. Wild or domestic canines have always preferred to sleep in den-like safe spots, and that is exactly what the crate provides. How often have you seen adult dogs that choose to sleep under a table or chair even though they have full run of the house? It's the den connection.

TIDY BOY

Clean by nature, dogs do not like to soil their dens, which in effect are their crates or sleeping quarters, and Basenjis are more fastidious about cleanliness than most dogs. Unless not feeling well, dogs will not defecate or urinate in their crates. Crate training capitalizes on the dog's natural desire to keep his den clean. Be conscientious about giving the puppy as many opportunities to relieve himself outdoors as possible. Reward the puppy for correct behavior. Praise him and pat him whenever he "goes" in the correct location. Even the tidiest of puppies can have potty accidents, so be patient and dedicate more energy to helping your puppy achieve a clean lifestyle.

In your "happy" voice, use the word "Crate" every time you put the pup into his den. If he's new to a crate, toss in a small biscuit for him to chase the first few times. At night, after he's been outside, he should sleep in his crate. The crate may be kept in his designated area at night or, if you want to be sure to hear those wake-up yips in the morning, put the crate in a corner of your bedroom. However, don't make any response whatsoever to whining or crying. If he's completely ignored, he'll settle down and get to sleep.

Good bedding for a young puppy is an old folded bath towel or an old blanket, something that is easily washable and disposable if necessary ("accidents" will happen!). Never put newspaper in the puppy's crate. Also those old ideas about adding a clock to replace his mother's heartbeat, or a hot-water bottle to replace her warmth, are just that—old ideas. The clock could drive the puppy nuts, and the hot-water bottle could end up as a very soggy waterbed! An extremely good breeder would have introduced your puppy to the crate by letting two pups sleep together for a couple of nights, followed by several nights alone. How thankful you will be if you found that breeder!

Safe toys in the pup's crate or area will keep him occupied, but monitor their condition closely. Discard any toys that show signs of being chewed to bits. Squeaky parts, bits of stuffing or plastic or any other small pieces can cause intestinal blockage or possibly choking if swallowed.

PROGRESSING WITH POTTY-TRAINING

After you've taken your puppy out and he has relieved himself in the area you've selected, he can have some free time with the family as long as there is someone responsible for watching him. That doesn't mean just someone in the same room who is watching TV or busy on the computer, but one person who is doing nothing other than keeping an eye on the pup, playing with him on the floor and helping him understand his position in the pack.

This first taste of freedom will let you begin to set the house rules. If you don't want the dog on the furniture, now is the time to prevent his first attempts to jump up onto the couch. The word to use in this case is "Off," not "Down." "Down" is the word you will use to teach the down position, which is something entirely different.

Most corrections at this stage come in the form of simply distracting the puppy. Instead of telling him "No" for "Don't chew the carpet," distract the chomping puppy with a toy and he'll forget about the carpet. With the Basenji, guiding him into proper behavior is more effective than scolding for improper behavior.

As you are playing with the pup, do not forget to watch him closely and pay attention to his body language. Whenever you see him begin to circle or sniff, take the puppy outside to relieve himself. If you are paper-training, put him back into his confined area on the newspapers. In either case, praise him as he eliminates while he actually is in the act of relieving himself. Three seconds after he has finished is too late! You'll be praising him for running toward you, or picking up a toy or whatever he may be doing at that moment, and that's not what you want to be praising

LEASH TRAINING

House-training and leash training go hand in hand, literally. When taking your puppy outside to do his business, lead him there on his leash. Unless an emergency potty run is called for, do not whisk the puppy up into your arms and take him outside. If you have a fenced yard, you have the advantage of letting the puppy loose to go out, but it's better to put the dog on the leash and take him to his designated place in the yard until he is reliably house-trained. Taking the puppy for a walk is the best way to house-train a dog. The dog will associate the walk with his time to relieve himself, and the exercise of walking stimulates the dog's bowels and bladder. Dogs that are not trained to relieve themselves on a walk may hold it until they get back home, which of course defeats half the purpose of the walk.

"Can I have some
privacy please?"

Very young
puppies relieve
themselves in the
same area in
which they are
kept, before they
are old enough to
venture outside
their quarters.
This ingenious
breeder has
provided a litter
box in the
puppy pen.

him for. Timing is a vital tool in all dog training. Use it.

Remove soiled newspapers immediately and replace them with clean ones. You may want to take a small piece of soiled paper and place it in the middle of the new clean papers, as the scent will attract him to that spot when it's time to go again. That scent attraction is why it's so important to clean up any messes made in the house by using a

product specially made to eliminate the odor of dog urine and droppings. Regular household cleansers won't do the trick. Pet shops sell the best pet deodorizers. Invest in the largest container you can find!

Scent attraction eventually will lead your pup to his chosen spot outdoors; this is the basis of outdoor training. When you take your puppy outside to relieve himself, use a one-word command such as "Outside" or "Go-potty" (that's one word to the puppy!) as you pick him up and attach his leash. Then put him down in his area. If for any reason you can't carry him, snap the leash on quickly and lead him to his spot. Now comes the hard part—hard for you, that is. Just stand there until he urinates and defecates. Move him a few feet in one direction or another if he's just sitting there looking at you, but remember that this is neither playtime nor time for a walk. This is strictly a business trip. Then, as he circles and squats (remember your timing!), give him a quiet "Good dog" as praise. If you start to jump for joy, ecstatic over his perform-ance, he'll do one of two things: either he will stop mid-stream, as it were, or he'll do it again for you—in the house—and expect you to be just as delighted!

Give him five minutes or so and, if he doesn't go in that time, take him back indoors to his confined area and try again in another ten minutes, or immediately if you see him sniffing and circling. By careful observation, you'll soon work out a successful schedule.

Accidents, by the way, are just that—accidents. Clean them up quickly and thoroughly,

Training begins as soon as your Basenji puppy comes home. Children must be instructed in how to handle the puppy and must always be supervised with the pup.

SOMEBODY TO BLAME

House-training a puppy can be frustrating for the puppy and the owner alike. The puppy does not instinctively understand the difference between defecating on the pavement outside and on the ceramic tile in the kitchen. He is confused and frightened by his human's exuberant reactions to his natural urges. The owner, arguably the more intelligent of the duo, is also frustrated that he cannot convince his puppy to obey his commands and instructions.

In frustration, the owner may struggle with the temptation to discipline the puppy, scold him or even strike him on the rear end. This will get you nowhere with the Basenji and will defeat your purpose in gaining your puppy's trust and respect. Don't blame your nine-week-old puppy. Blame yourself for not being 100% consistent in the puppy's lessons and routine. The lesson here is simple: try harder and your puppy will succeed.

---

without comment, after the puppy has been taken outside to finish his business and then put back into his area or crate. If you witness an accident in progress, say "No!" in a stern voice and get the pup outdoors immediately. No punishment is needed. You and your puppy are just learning each other's language, and sometimes it's easy to miss a puppy's message. Chalk it up to experience and watch more closely from now on.

KEEPING THE PACK ORDERLY

Discipline is a form of training that brings order to life. For example, military discipline is what allows the soldiers in an army to work as one. Discipline is a form of teaching and, in dogs, is the basis of how the successful pack operates. Each member knows his place in the pack and all respect the leader, or Alpha dog. It is essential for your puppy that you establish this type of relationship, with you as the Alpha, or leader. It is a form of social coexistence that all canines recognize and accept. Discipline, therefore, is never to be confused with punishment. When you teach your puppy how you want him to behave, and he behaves properly and you praise him for it, you are disciplining

Having trouble keeping your Basenji's attention? Produce a treat and see what happens!

KEEP IT SIMPLE—AND FUN

Practicing obedience is not a military drill. Keep your lessons simple, interesting and user-friendly. Fun breaks help you both. Spend two minutes or ten teaching your puppy, but practice only as long as your dog enjoys what he's doing and is focused on pleasing you. If he's bored or distracted, stop the training session after any correct response (always end on a high note!). After a few minutes of playtime, you can go back to "hitting the books."

him with a form of positive reinforcement, the best type of training for the Basenji.

For a dog, rewards come in the form of praise, a smile, a cheerful tone of voice, a few friendly pats or a rub of the ears. Rewards are also small food treats. Obviously, that does not mean bits of regular dog food. Instead, treats are very small bits of special things like cheese or pieces of soft dog treats. The idea is to reward the dog with something very small that he can taste and swallow, providing instant positive reinforcement. If he has to take time to chew a crunchy dog biscuit, by the time he is finished he will have forgotten what he did to earn it.

Your puppy should never be physically punished. The displeasure shown on your face and in your voice is sufficient to signal to the pup that he has done something wrong. He wants to please everyone higher up on the social ladder, especially his leader, so a scowl and harsh voice will take care of the error. Growling out the word "Shame!" when the pup is caught in the act of doing something wrong is better than the repetitive "No." Some dogs hear "No" so often that they begin to think it's their name! By the way, do not use the dog's name when you're correcting him. His name is reserved to get his attention for something pleasant about to take place.

There are punishments that have nothing to do with you. For example, your dog may think that

Cat meets "cat-like" dog! As with dog-to-dog introductions, introductions between the Basenji and any other animal must be made with care.

chasing cats is one reason for his existence. You can try to stop it as much as you like but without success, because it's such fun for the dog. But one good hissing, spitting swipe of a cat's claws across the dog's nose will put an end to the game forever. Intervene only when your dog's eyeball is seriously at risk. Cat scratches can cause permanent damage to an innocent but annoying puppy.

PUPPY KINDERGARTEN

COLLAR AND LEASH
Before you begin your Basenji puppy's education, he must be used to his collar and leash. Choose a collar for your puppy that is secure, but not heavy or bulky. He won't enjoy training if

---

BASIC PRINCIPLES OF DOG TRAINING

1. Start training early. A young puppy is ready, willing and able.
2. Timing is your all-important tool. Praise at the exact time that the dog responds correctly. Pay close attention.
3. Patience is almost as important as timing!
4. Repeat! The same word has to mean the same thing every time.
5. In the beginning, praise all correct behavior verbally, along with treats and petting, then eventually use verbal praise and petting only. Regardless, keep it positive.

to take the puppy outside to relieve himself is shorter because you don't want him to roam away from his area. The shorter leash will also be the one to use when you walk the puppy.

If you've been wise enough to enroll in a Puppy Kindergarten training class, suggestions will be made as to the best collar and leash for your young puppy. I say "wise" because your puppy will be in a class with puppies in his age range (up to five months old) of all breeds and sizes. It's the perfect way for him to learn the

Since this Basenji has a table full of treats at mouth level, he's decided to "reward" himself. Sweet treats, though, are not so sweet— eating chocolate can even kill a dog. Keep all "people food" out of your dog's reach.

he's uncomfortable. A flat buckle collar is fine for everyday wear and for initial puppy training. For older dogs, there are several types of training collars such as the martingale, also called the "Greyhound collar" and used with many sighthounds, which is a double loop that tightens slightly around the neck, or the head collar, which is similar to a horse's halter. The Basenji does not require the physical correction of a choke collar.

A lightweight 6-foot woven cotton or nylon training leash is preferred by most trainers because it is easy to fold up in your hand and comfortable to hold because there is a certain amount of give to it. There are lessons where the dog will start off 6 feet away from you at the end of the leash. The leash used

TIME TO PLAY!

Playtime can happen both indoors and out. A young puppy is growing so rapidly that he needs sleep more than he needs a lot of physical exercise. Puppies get sufficient exercise on their own just through normal puppy activity. Monitor play with young children so you can remove the puppy when he's had enough, or calm the kids if they get too rowdy. Almost all puppies love to chase after a toy you've thrown, and you can turn your games into educational activities. Every time your puppy brings the toy back to you, say "Give it" (or "Drop it") followed by "Good dog" and throwing it again. If he's reluctant to give it to you, offer a small treat so that he drops the toy as he takes the treat. He will soon get the idea.

right way (and the wrong way) to interact with other dogs as well as their people. You cannot teach your puppy how to interpret another dog's sign language. For a first-time puppy owner, these socialization classes are invaluable. For experienced dog owners, they are a real boon to further training.

ATTENTION

You've been using the dog's name since the minute you collected him from the breeder, so you should be able to get his attention by saying his name—with a big smile and in an excited tone of voice. His response will be the puppy equivalent of "Here I am! What are we going to do?" Your immediate response (if you haven't guessed by now) is "Good dog." Rewarding him at the moment he pays attention to you teaches him the proper way to respond when he hears his name.

EXERCISES FOR A BASIC CANINE EDUCATION

THE SIT EXERCISE

There are several ways to teach the puppy to sit. The first one is to catch him whenever he is about to sit and, as his backside nears the floor, say "Sit, good dog!" That's positive reinforcement and, if your timing is sharp,

---

SIT AROUND THE HOUSE

"Sit" is the command you'll use most often. Your pup objects when placed in a sit with your hands, so try the "bringing the food up under his chin" method. Better still, catch him in the act! Your dog will sit on his own many times throughout the day, so let him know that he's doing the "Sit" by rewarding him. Praise him and have him sit for everything—toys, connecting his leash, his dinner, before going out the door, etc.

---

he will learn that what he's doing at that second is connected to your saying "Sit" and that you think he's clever for doing it!

Another method is to start with the puppy on his leash in front of you. Show him a treat in the palm of your right hand. Bring your hand up under his nose and, almost in slow motion, move your hand up and back so his nose goes up in the air and his head tilts back as he follows the treat in your hand. At that point, he will have to either sit or fall over, so as his back legs buckle under, say "Sit, good dog," and then give him the treat and lots of praise. You may have to begin with your hand lightly running up his chest, actually lifting his chin up until he sits. Some (usually older) dogs require gentle pressure on their hindquarters with the left hand,

Use treats and a gentle tone of voice to convince your Basenji that it's ok to "get down."

verbal command and the motion of the hand are signals for the sit. Your puppy is watching you almost more than he is listening to you, so what you do is just as important as what you say.

Don't save any of these drills only for training sessions. Use them as much as possible at odd times during a normal day. The dog should always sit before being given his food dish. He should sit to let you go through a doorway first, when the doorbell rings or when you stop to speak to someone on the street.

in which case the dog should be on your left side. Puppies generally do not appreciate this physical dominance.

After a few times, you should be able to show the dog a treat in the open palm of your hand, raise your hand waist-high as you say "Sit" and have him sit. You thus will have taught him two things at the same time. Both the

THE DOWN EXERCISE

Before beginning to teach the down command, you must consider how the dog feels about this exercise. To him, "down" is a submissive position. Being flat on the floor with you standing over him is not his idea of fun. It's up to you to let him know that, while it may not be fun, the reward of your approval is worth his effort.

Start with the puppy on your left side in a sit position. Hold the leash right above his collar in your left hand. Have an extra-special treat, such as a small piece of cooked chicken or hotdog, in your right hand. Place it at the end of the pup's nose and steadily move your hand down and forward along the ground. Hold the leash to prevent a sudden lunge for the food. As

---

READY, SIT, GO!

On your marks, get set: train! Most professional trainers agree that the sit command is the place to start your dog's formal education. Sitting is a natural posture for most dogs, and they respond to the sit exercise willingly and readily. For every lesson, begin with the sit command so that you start out on a successful note; likewise, you should practice the sit command at the end of every lesson as well, because you always want to end on a high note.

the puppy goes into the down position, say "Down" very gently.

The difficulty with this exercise is twofold: it's both the submissive aspect and the fact that most people say the word "Down" as if they were a drill sergeant in charge of recruits. So issue the command sweetly, give him the treat and have the pup maintain the down position for several seconds. If he tries to get up immediately, place your hands on his shoulders and press down gently, giving him a very quiet "Good dog." As you progress with this lesson, increase the "down time" until he will hold it until you say "Okay" (his cue for release). Practice this one in the house at various times throughout the day.

By increasing the length of time during which the dog must maintain the down position, you'll find many uses for it. For example, he can lie at your feet in the vet's office or anywhere that both of you have to wait, when you are on the phone, while the family is eating and so forth. If you progress to training for competitive obedience, he'll already be all set for the exercise called the "long down."

THE STAY EXERCISE

You can teach your Basenji to stay in the sit, down and stand positions. To teach the sit/stay, have the dog sit on your left side.

Hold the leash at waist level in your left hand and let the dog know that you have a treat in your closed right hand. Step forward on your right foot as you say "Stay." Immediately turn and stand directly in front of the dog, keeping your right hand up high

> ### SWEET AND LOW DOWN
> "Down" is a harsh-sounding word and a submissive posture in dog body language, thus presenting two obstacles in teaching the down command. When the dog is about to flop down on his own, tell him "Good down." Pups that are not good about being handled learn better by having food lowered in front of them. A dog that trusts you can be gently guided into position. When you give the command "Down," be sure to say it sweetly!

Use a hand signal to give the down/stay command. Say "Stay" in a calm, firm tone of voice.

so he'll keep his eye on the treat hand and maintain the sit position for a count of five. Return to your original position and offer the reward.

Increase the length of the sit/stay each time until the dog can hold it for at least 30 seconds without moving. After about a week of success, move out on your right foot and take two steps before turning to face the dog. Give the "Stay" hand signal (left palm back toward the dog's head) as you leave. He gets the treat when you return and he holds

TIPS FOR
TRAINING AND SAFETY

1. Whether on- or off-leash, practice only in a fenced area.
2. Remove the training collar when the training session is over.
3. Don't try to break up a dog-fight.
4. "Come," "Leave it" and "Wait" are safety commands.
5. The dog belongs in a crate or behind a barrier when riding in the car.
6. Don't ignore the dog's first sign of aggression. Aggression only gets worse, so take it seriously.
7. Keep the faces of children and dogs separated.
8. Pay attention to what the dog is chewing.
9. Keep the vet's number near your phone.
10. "Okay" is a useful release command.

the sit/stay. Increase the distance that you walk away from him before turning until you reach the length of your training leash. But don't rush it! Go back to the beginning if he moves before he should. No matter what the lesson, never be upset by having to back up for a few days. The repetition and practice are what will make your dog reliable in these commands. It won't do any good to move on to something more difficult if the command is not mastered at the easier levels. Above all, even if you do get frustrated, never let your puppy know! Always keep a positive, upbeat attitude during training, which will transmit to your dog for positive results.

The down/stay is taught in the same way once the dog is completely reliable and steady with the down command. Again, don't rush it. With the dog in the down position on your left side, step out on your right foot as you say "Stay." Return by walking around in back of the dog and into your original position. While you are training, it's okay to murmur something like "Hold on" to encourage him to stay put. When the dog will stay without moving when you are at a distance of 3 or 4 feet, begin to increase the length of time before you return. Be sure he holds the down on your return until you say "Okay." At that point, he gets his treat—just so he'll remember for next time that it's not over until it's over.

THE COME EXERCISE

No command is more important to the safety of your Basenji than "come." It is what you should say every single time you see the puppy running toward you: "Bongo, come! Good dog." During playtime, run a few feet away from the puppy and turn and tell him to "come" as he is already running to you. You can go so far as to teach your puppy two things at once if you squat down and hold out your arms. As the pup gets close to you and you're saying "Good dog," bring your right arm in about waist

high. Now he's also learning the hand signal, an excellent device should you be on the phone when you need to get him to come to you.

When the puppy responds to your well-timed "Come," try it with the puppy on the training leash. This time, catch him off-guard, while he's sniffing a leaf or watching a bird: "Bongo, come!" You may have to pause for a split second after his name to be sure you have his attention. If the puppy shows any sign of

COME AND GET IT!

The come command is your dog's safety signal. Until he is 99% perfect in responding, don't use the come command if you cannot enforce it. Practice on leash with treats or squeakers, or whenever the dog is running to you. Never call him to come to you if he is to be corrected for a misdemeanor. Reward the dog with a treat and happy praise whenever he comes to you.

confusion, give the leash a mild jerk and take a couple of steps backward. Do not repeat the command. In this case, you should say "Good come" as he reaches you.

That's the number-one rule of training. Each command word is given just once. Anything more is nagging. You'll also notice that all commands are one word only. Even when they are actually two words, you say them as one.

Never call the dog to come to you—with or without his name—if you are angry or intend to correct him for some misbehavior. When correcting the pup, you go to him. Your dog must always connect "come" with something pleasant and with your approval; then you can rely on his response.

Puppies, like children, have notoriously short attention spans, so don't overdo it with any of the training. Keep each lesson short. Break it up with a quick run around the yard or a ball toss, repeat the lesson and quit as soon as the pup gets it right. That way, you will always end with a "good dog."

Life isn't perfect and neither are puppies. A time will come, often around 10 months of age, when he'll become "selectively deaf" or choose to "forget" his name. He may respond by wagging his tail (and even seeming to smile at you) with a look that says "Make me!" Laugh, throw his favorite toy and skip the lesson you had planned. Pups will be pups!

THE HEEL EXERCISE

The second most important command to teach, after the come, is the heel. When you are walking your growing puppy, you need to be in control. Besides, it looks terrible to be pulled and yanked down the street, and it's not much fun either. Your eight- to ten-week-old puppy will probably follow you everywhere,

---

FEAR AGGRESSION

Of the several types of aggression, the one brought on by fear is the most difficult for people to comprehend and to deal with. Aggression to protect food, or any object the dog perceives as his, is more easily understood. Fear aggression is quite different. The dog shows fear, generally for no apparent reason. He backs off, cowers or hides under the bed. If he's on lead, he will hide behind your leg and lash out unexpectedly. No matter how you approach him, he will bite. A fear-biter attacks with great speed and instantly retreats. Don't shout at him or go near him. Don't coddle, sympathize or try to protect him. To him, that's a reward. As with other forms of aggression, get professional help.

but that's his natural instinct, not your control over the situation. However, any time he does follow you, you can say "Heel" and be ahead of the game, as he will learn to associate this command with the action of following you before you even begin teaching him to heel.

There is a very precise, almost military, procedure for teaching your dog to heel. As with all other obedience training, begin with the dog on your left side. He will be in a very nice sit and you will have the training leash across your chest. Hold the loop and folded leash in your right hand. Pick up the slack leash above the dog in your left hand and hold it loosely at your side. Step out on your left foot as you say "Heel." If the puppy does not move, give a gentle tug or pat your left leg to get him started. If he surges ahead of you, stop and pull him back gently until he is at your side. Tell him to sit and begin again.

Walk a few steps and stop while the puppy is correctly beside you. Tell him to sit and give mild verbal praise. (More enthusiastic praise will encourage him to think the lesson is over.) Repeat the lesson, increasing the number of steps you take only as long as the dog is heeling nicely beside you. When you end the lesson, have him hold the sit, then give him

LET'S GO!

Many people use "Let's go" instead of "Heel" when teaching their dogs to behave on lead. It sounds more like fun! When beginning to teach the heel, whatever command you use, always step off on your left foot. That's the one next to the dog, who is on your left side, in case you've forgotten. Keep a loose leash. When the dog pulls ahead, stop, bring him back and begin again. Use treats to guide him around turns.

Don't push it if your Basenji looks like he's had enough. End the lesson and try again later.

the "Okay" to let him know that this is the end of the lesson. Praise him so that he knows he did a good job.

The cure for excessive pulling (a common problem) is to stop when the dog is no more than 2 or 3 feet ahead of you. Guide him back into position and begin again. With a really determined puller, try switching to a head collar. This will automatically turn the pup's head toward you so you can bring him back easily to the heel position. Give quiet, reassuring praise every time the leash goes slack and he's staying with you.

RIGHT CLICK ON YOUR DOG

With three clicks, the dolphin jumps through the hoop. Wouldn't it be nice to have a dog who could obey wordless commands that easily? Clicker training actually was developed by dolphin trainers and today is used on dogs with great success. You can buy a clicker at a pet shop or pet-supply outlet, and then you'll be off and clicking. This method has proven quite successful with Basenjis.

You can click your dog into learning new commands, shaping or conditioning his behavior and solving bad habits. The clicker, used in conjunction with a treat, is an extension of positive reinforcement. The dog begins to recognize your happy clicking, and this becomes a sufficient reward. The dog is conditioned to follow your hand with the clicker, just as he would follow your hand with a treat. To discourage the dog from inappropriate behavior (like jumping up or barking), you can use the clicker to set a timeframe and then click and reward the dog once he's waited the allotted time without jumping up or barking.

Staying and heeling can take a lot out of a dog, so provide playtime and free-running exercise to shake off the stress when the lessons are over. You don't want him to associate training with all work and no fun.

TAPERING OFF TIDBITS

Your dog has been watching you—and the hand that treats—throughout all of his lessons, and now it's time to break the treat habit. Begin by giving him treats at the end of each lesson only. Then start to give a treat after the end of only some of the lessons. At the end of every lesson, as well as during the lessons, be consistent with the praise. Your pup now doesn't know whether he'll get a treat or not, but he should keep performing well just in case! Finally, you will stop

> ### OKAY!
> This is the signal that tells your dog that he can quit whatever he was doing. Use "Okay" to end a session on a correct response to a command. (Never end on an incorrect response.) Lots of praise follows. People use "Okay" a lot and it has other uses for dogs, too. Your dog is barking. You say, "Okay! Come!" "Okay" signals him to stop the barking activity and "Come" allows him to come to you for a "Good dog."

giving treat rewards entirely. Save them for something brand-new that you want to teach him. Keep up the praise and you'll always have a "good dog."

OBEDIENCE CLASSES

The advantages of an obedience class are that your dog will have

Basenjis are very agile dogs. They not only adapt to agility training, they actually enjoy it.

to learn amid the distractions of other people and dogs and that your mistakes will be quickly corrected by the trainer. Teaching your dog along with a qualified instructor and other handlers who may have more dog experience than you is another plus of the class environment. The instructor and other handlers can help you to find the most efficient way of teaching your dog a command or exercise. It's often easier to learn by other people's mistakes than your own. You will also learn all of the requirements for competitive obedience trials, in which you can earn titles and go on to advanced jumping and retrieving exercises, which are fun for many dogs. Obedience classes build the foundation needed for many other canine activities (in which we humans are allowed to participate, too!).

Lure coursing, like dog races, are exciting for dog and owner. A Basenji flying by in his "running silks" is a beautiful sight to behold.

TRAINING FOR OTHER ACTIVITIES

Once your dog has basic obedience under his collar and is 12 months of age, you can enter the world of agility training. Dogs think agility is pure fun, like being turned loose in an amusement park full of obstacles! Basenjis are quick, agile and alert, able to participate successfully in many areas of the dog sport with proper training. Controlled lure-coursing is an excellent option to investigate. It is a thrill to see the Basenjis, garbed in brightly colored vests, chasing a pseudo-bunny or the like along a track or field. Contact the American Sighthound Field Association or a local breed club to find out about lure-coursing events in your area. Even if your Basenji is not too keen on participating, these events make enjoyable outings for the entire family as spectators (Basenji included!).

Learning to heel is essential for all dogs. If yours is a show Basenji, you will find this command to be especially helpful as you gait your dog in the ring, a requirement as the judge assesses the dog's movement.

For those who like to volunteer, there is the wonderful feeling of owning a therapy dog and visiting hospices, nursing homes and veterans' homes to bring smiles, comfort and companionship to those who live there. Consider also the possibility of teaching your Basenji to hunt. The breed has been used on partridge, rabbit and even duck, working in any cover. It can find, flush, drive and game—a truly versatile hunter. Around the house, your Basenji can be taught to do some simple chores. The kids can teach the dog all kinds of tricks, from playing hide-and-seek to balancing a biscuit on his nose. A family dog is what rounds out the family. Everything he does beyond sitting in your lap or gazing lovingly at you represents the bonus of owning a dog.

DON'T STRESS ME OUT

Your dog doesn't have to deal with paying the bills, the daily commute, PTA meetings and the like, but, believe it or not, there's a lot of stress in a dog's world. Stress can be caused by the owner's impatient demeanor and his angry or harsh corrections. If your dog cringes when you reach for his training collar, he's stressed. An older dog is sometimes stressed out when he goes to a new home. No matter what the cause, put off all training until he's over it. If he's going through a fear period—shying away from people, trembling when spoken to, avoiding eye contact or hiding under furniture—wait to resume training. Naturally you'd also postpone your lessons if the dog were sick, and the same goes for you. Show some compassion.

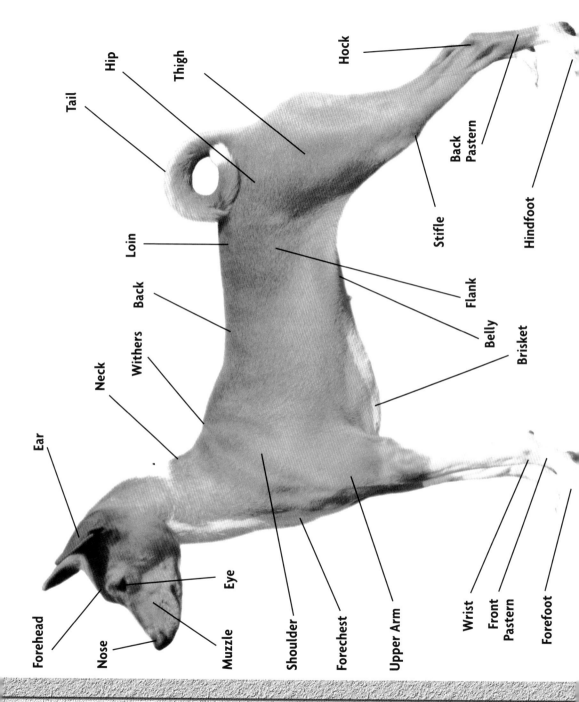

Tail

Hip

Thigh

Hock

Back Pastern

Stifle

Hindfoot

Loin

Back

Flank

Belly

Brisket

Withers

Neck

Ear

Eye

Forehead

Nose

Muzzle

Shoulder

Forechest

Upper Arm

Wrist

Front Pastern

Forefoot

PHYSICAL STRUCTURE OF THE BASENJI

BASENJI

BY LOWELL ACKERMAN DVM, DACVD

HEALTHCARE FOR A LIFETIME

When you own a dog, you become his healthcare advocate over his entire lifespan, as well as being the one to shoulder the financial burden of such care. Accordingly, it is worthwhile to focus on prevention rather than treatment, as you and your pet will both be happier.

Of course, the best place to have begun your program of preventive healthcare is with the initial purchase or adoption of your dog. There is no way of guaranteeing that your new furry friend is free of medical problems, but there are some things you can do to improve your odds. You certainly should have done adequate research into the Basenji and have selected your puppy carefully rather than buying on impulse. Health issues aside, a large number of pet abandonment and relinquishment cases arise from a mismatch between pet needs and owner expectations. This is entirely preventable with appropriate planning and finding a good breeder.

Regarding healthcare issues specifically, it is very difficult to make blanket statements about where to acquire a problem-free pet, but, again, a reputable breeder is your best bet. In an ideal situation, you have learned about the potential breed-specific problems, and you have the opportunity to see both parents, get references from other owners of the breeder's pups and see genetic-testing documentation for several generations of the litter's ancestors. At the very least, you must thoroughly investigate the Basenji and the problems inherent in the breed, as well as the genetic testing available to screen for

A four-month-old Basenji in front of an abdominal x-ray at the vet's office. You should select a local veterinarian before you bring your Basenji home, and your puppy should be examined as soon as possible after your acquisition.

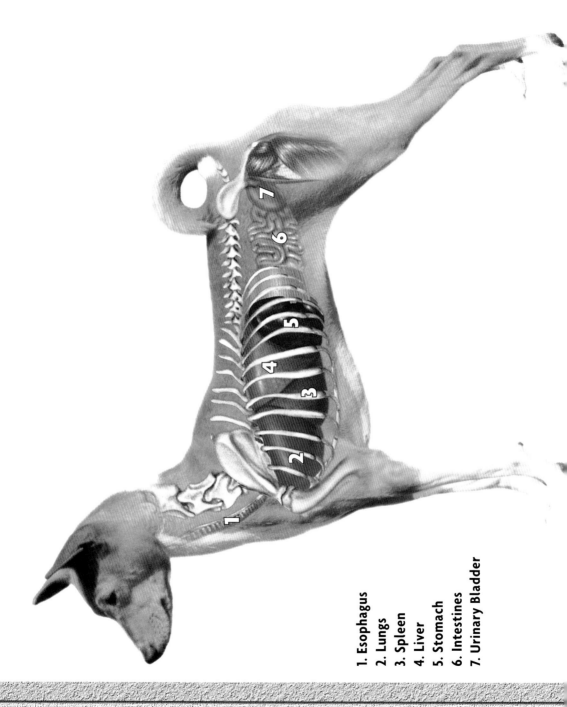

1. Esophagus
2. Lungs
3. Spleen
4. Liver
5. Stomach
6. Intestines
7. Urinary Bladder

INTERNAL ORGANS OF THE BASENJI

those problems. Genetic testing offers some important benefits, but testing is available for only a few disorders in a relatively small number of breeds and is not available for some of the most common genetic diseases, such as hip dysplasia, cataracts, epilepsy, cardiomyopathy, etc. This area of research is indeed exciting and increasingly important, and

Training your Basenji means not only house-training and teaching him the rules of the home but also instructing how to behave properly in any given situation. This Basenji sits politely to take medication.

TAKING YOUR DOG'S TEMPERATURE

It is important to know how to take your dog's temperature at times when you think he may be ill. It's not the most enjoyable task, but it can be done without too much difficulty. It's easier with a helper, preferably someone with whom the dog is friendly, so that one of you can hold the dog while the other inserts the thermometer.

Before inserting the thermometer, coat the end with petroleum jelly. Insert the thermometer slowly and gently into the dog's rectum about one inch. Wait for the reading, about two minutes. Be sure to remove the thermometer carefully and clean it thoroughly after each use.

For most dogs, normal body temperature is between 100.5 and 102.5 degrees F. However, the Basenji's temperature tends to be about 1 degree lower. Immediate veterinary attention is required if the dog's temperature is below 98 or above 103 degrees F.

advances will continue to be made each year. In fact, recent research has shown that there is an equivalent dog gene for 75% of known human genes, so research done in either species is likely to benefit the other.

We've also discussed that evaluating the behavioral nature of your Basenji and that of his immediate family members is an important part of the selection process that cannot be underestimated or overemphasized. It is sometimes difficult to evaluate temperament in puppies because certain behavioral tendencies, such as some forms of aggression, may not be immediately evident.

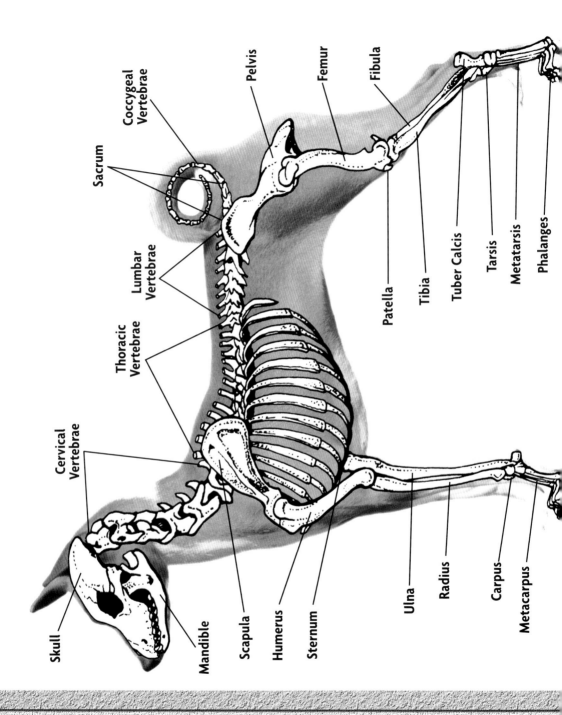

Coccygeal Vertebrae

Pelvis

Femur

Fibula

Sacrum

Lumbar Vertebrae

Thoracic Vertebrae

Patella

Tibia

Tuber Calcis

Tarsis

Metatarsis

Phalanges

Cervical Vertebrae

Skull

Mandible

Scapula

Humerus

Sternum

Ulna

Radius

Carpus

Metacarpus

SKELETAL STRUCTURE OF THE BASENJI

More dogs are euthanized each year for behavioral reasons than for all medical conditions combined, so it is critical to take temperament issues seriously. Start with a well-balanced, friendly companion and put the time and effort into proper socialization, and you will both be rewarded with a lifelong valued relationship.

Assuming that you have started off with a pup from healthy, sound stock, you then become responsible for helping your veterinarian keep your pet healthy. Some crucial things happen before you even bring your puppy home. Parasite control typically begins at two weeks of age, and vaccinations typically begin at six to eight weeks of age. A pre-pubertal evaluation is typically scheduled for about six months of age. At this time, a dental evaluation is done (since the adult teeth are now in), heartworm prevention is started and neutering or spaying is most commonly done.

It is critical to commence regular dental care at home if you have not already done so. It may not sound very important, but most dogs have active periodontal disease by four years of age if they don't have their teeth cleaned regularly at home, not just at their veterinary exams. Dental problems lead to more than just bad "doggie breath." Gum disease

DOGGIE DENTAL DON'TS

A veterinary dental exam is necessary if you notice one or any combination of the following in your dog:
- Broken, loose or missing teeth
- Loss of appetite (which could be due to mouth pain or illness caused by infection)
- Gum abnormalities, including redness, swelling and bleeding
- Drooling, with or without blood
- Yellowing of the teeth or gumline, indicating tartar
- Bad breath

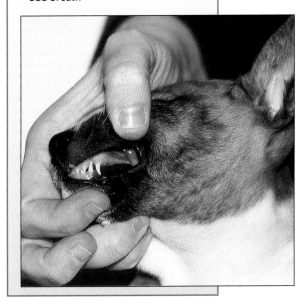

can have very serious medical consequences. If you start using canine dental-care products—brushing your dog's teeth and using antiseptic rinses—from a young age, your dog will be accustomed to it and will not

Basenjis are sensitive, intelligent dogs that require dedicated, educated owners to provide them with proper care.

resist. The results will be healthy dentition, which your pet will need to enjoy a long, healthy life.

Most dogs are considered adults at a year of age, although some larger breeds still have some filling out to do up to about two or so years old. Even individual dogs within each breed have different healthcare requirements, so work with your veterinarian to determine what will be needed and what your role should be. This doctor-client relationship is important, because as vaccination guidelines change, there may not be an annual "vaccine visit" scheduled. You must make sure that you see your veterinarian at least annually, even if no vaccines are due, because this is the best opportunity to coordinate health-care activities and to make sure that no medical issues creep by unaddressed. Certain problems, like Fanconi and some eye disorders, do not occur until the dog's adult years, so ongoing testing is advised.

When your Basenji reaches three-quarters of his anticipated lifespan, he is considered a "senior" and likely requires some special care. In general, if you've been taking great care of your canine companion throughout his formative and adult years, the transition to senior status should be a smooth one. Age is not a disease, and as long as everything is functioning as it should, there

is no reason why most of late adulthood should not be rewarding for both you and your pet. This is especially true if you have tended to the details, such as regular veterinary visits, proper dental care, excellent nutrition and management of bone, joint and weight issues.

At this stage in your Basenji's life, your veterinarian may want to schedule visits twice yearly, instead of once, to run some laboratory screenings, electrocar-diograms and the like, and to change the diet to something more digestible. Catching problems early is the best way to manage them effectively. Treating the early stages of heart disease is so much easier than trying to intervene when there is more significant damage to the heart muscle.

Finding a good vet, who treats your Basenji kindly and is knowledgeable about the breed's health, is one of the most important things you can do for your Basenji.

THE EYES HAVE IT!
Eye disease is more prevalent among dogs than most people think, ranging from slight infections that are easily treated to serious complications that can lead to permanent sight loss. Eye diseases need veterinary attention in their early stages to prevent irreparable damage. This list provides descriptions of some common eye diseases:

Cataracts: Symptoms are white or gray discoloration of the eye lens and pupil, which causes fuzzy or completely obscured vision. Surgical treatment is required to remove the damaged lens and replace it with an artificial one.

Conjunctivitis: An inflammation of the mucus membrane that lines the eye socket, leaving the eyes red and puffy with excessive discharge. This condition is easily treated with antibiotics.

Corneal damage: The cornea is the transparent covering of the iris and pupil. Injuries are difficult to detect, but manifest themselves in surface abnormality, redness, pain and discharge. Most infections of the cornea are treated with antibiotics and require immediate medical attention.

Dry eye: This condition is caused by deficient production of tears that lubricate and protect the eye surface. A telltale sign is yellow-green discharge. Left undiagnosed, your dog will experience considerable pain, infections and possibly blindness. Dry eye is commonly treated with antibiotics, although more advanced cases may require surgery.

Glaucoma: This is caused by excessive fluid pressure in the eye. Symptoms are red eyes, gray or blue discoloration, pain, enlarged eyeballs and loss of vision. Antibiotics sometimes help, but surgery may be needed.

Similarly, managing the beginning of kidney problems is fairly routine if there is no significant kidney damage. Other problems, like cognitive dysfunction (similar to senility and Alzheimer's disease), cancer, diabetes and arthritis, are more common in older dogs, but all can be treated to help the dog live as many happy, comfortable years as possible. Just as in people, medical management is more effective (and less expensive) when you catch things early.

SELECTING A VETERINARIAN
There is probably no more important decision that you will make regarding your pet's health-care than the selection of his doctor. Your pet's veterinarian will be a pediatrician, family-practice physician and gerontologist, depending on the dog's life stage, and will be the individual who makes recommendations regarding issues such as when specialists need to be consulted, when diagnostic testing and/or therapeutic intervention is needed and when you will need to seek

YOUR DOG NEEDS TO VISIT THE VET IF:

- He has ingested a toxin such as antifreeze or a toxic plant; in these cases, administer first aid and call the vet right away
- His teeth are discolored, loose or missing or he has sores or other signs of infection or abnormality in the mouth
- He has been vomiting, has had diarrhea or has been constipated for over 24 hours; call immediately if you notice blood
- He has refused food for over 24 hours
- His eating habits, water intake or toilet habits have noticeably changed; if you have noticed weight gain or weight loss
- He shows symptoms of bloat, which requires *immediate* attention
- He is salivating excessively
- He has a lump in his throat
- He has a lump or bump anywhere on the body
- He is very lethargic
- He appears to be in pain or otherwise has trouble chewing or swallowing
- His skin loses elasticity

Of course, there will be other instances in which a visit to the vet is necessary; these are just some of the signs that could be indicative of serious problems that need to be caught as early as possible.

outside emergency and critical-care services. Your vet will act as your advocate and liaison throughout these processes.

Everyone has his own idea about what to look for in a vet, an individual who will play a big role in his dog's (and, of course, his own) life for many years to come. For some, it is the compassionate caregiver with whom they hope to develop a professional relationship to span the lifetime of their dogs and even their future pets. For others, they are seeking a clinician with keen diagnostic and therapeutic insight who can deliver state-of-the-art healthcare. Still others need a veterinary facility that is open evenings and weekends, or is in close proximity or provides mobile veterinary services, to accommodate their schedules; these people may not much mind that their dogs might see different veterinarians on each visit. Just as we have different reasons for selecting our own healthcare professionals (e.g., covered by insurance plan, expert in field, convenient location, etc.), we should not expect that there is a one-size-fits-all recommendation for selecting a veterinarian and veterinary practice. The best advice is to be honest in your assessment of what you expect from a veterinary practice and to conscientiously research the options in your area. You will quickly appreciate that not all

HIT ME WITH A HOT SPOT

What is a hot spot? Technically known as pyotraumatic dermatitis, a hot spot is an infection on the dog's coat, usually by the rear end, under the tail or on a leg, which the dog inflicts upon himself. The dog licks and bites the itchy spot until it becomes inflamed and infected. The hot spot can range in size from the circumference of a grape to the circumference of an apple. Provided that the hot spot is not related to a deeper bacterial infection, it can be treated topically by clipping the area, cleaning the sore and giving prednisone. For bacterial infections, antibiotics are required. In some cases, an Elizabethan collar is required to keep the dog from further irritating the hot spot. The itching can intensify and the pain becomes worse. Medicated shampoos and cool compresses, drying agents and topical steroids may be prescribed by your vet as well.

Hot spots can be caused by fleas, an allergy, an ear infection, anal sac problems, mange or a foreign irritant. Likewise, they can be linked to psychoses. The underlying problem must be addressed in addition to the hot spot itself.

ago, a single veterinarian would attempt to manage all medical and surgical issues as they arose. That was often problematic, because veterinarians are trained in many species and many diseases, and it was just impossible for general veterinary practitioners to be experts in every species, every field and every ailment. However, just as in the human healthcare fields, specialization has allowed general practitioners to concentrate on primary healthcare delivery, especially wellness and the prevention of infectious diseases, and to utilize a network of specialists to assist in the management of conditions that require specific expertise and experience. Thus there are now many types of veterinary specialists, including dermatologists, cardiologists, ophthalmologists, surgeons, internists, oncologists, neurologists, behaviorists, criticalists and others to help primary-care veterinarians deal with complicated medical challenges. In most cases, specialists see cases referred by primary-care veterinarians, make diagnoses and set up management plans. From there, the animals' ongoing care is returned to their primary-care veterinarians. This important team approach to your pet's medical-care needs has provided opportunities for advanced care and an unparalleled level of quality to be delivered.

veterinary practices are the same, and you will be happiest with one that truly meets your needs.

There is another point to be considered in the selection of veterinary services. Not that long

With all of the opportunities for your Basenji to receive high-quality veterinary medical care, there is another topic that needs to be addressed at the same time—cost. It's been said that you can have excellent healthcare or inexpensive healthcare, but never both; this is as true in veterinary medicine as it is in human medicine. While veterinary costs are a fraction of what the same services cost in the human health-care arena, it is still difficult to deal with unanticipated medical costs, especially since they can easily creep into hundreds or even thousands of dollars if specialists or emergency services become involved. However, there are ways of managing these risks. The easiest is to buy pet health insurance and realize that its foremost purpose is not to cover routine healthcare visits but rather to serve as an umbrella for those rainy days when your pet needs medical care and you don't want to worry about whether or not you can afford that care.

Pet insurance policies are very cost-effective (and very inexpensive by human health-insurance standards), but make sure that you buy the policy long before you intend to use it (preferably starting in puppyhood, because coverage will exclude pre-existing conditions) and that you are actually buying an indemnity insurance plan from an insurance

FOOD ALLERGY

Severe itching, leading to bald patches and open sores on the feet, face, ears, armpits and groin, could be caused by a food allergy. Studies indicate that up to 10% of dogs suffer from food allergies. Dogs who suffer from chronic ear problems may actually have a food allergy. Unfortunately, there are no tests available to determine whether your dog definitely suffers from a food allergy. The dog will be miserable and you will be frustrated and stressed.

Take the problem into your own hands and kitchen. Select a type of meat that your dog is not getting from his existing diet, perhaps white fish, lamb or venison, and prepare a home-cooked food. The food should consist of two parts carbohydrate (rice, pasta or potatoes) and one part protein (the chosen meat). It's better not to start with soy as the protein source unless all of the meats cause a reaction.

Monitor your dog's intake carefully. He must eat only your prepared meal without any treats or side-trips to the garbage can. All family members (and visiting friends) must be informed of the plan. After four or five weeks on the new diet, you will reintroduce a portion of his original diet to determine whether this food is the cause of the skin irritation (or other reactions). Once the dog reacts to the change in diet, resume the new diet. Make dietary modifications every two weeks and keep careful records of any reactions the dog has to the diet.

COMMON INFECTIOUS DISEASES

Let's discuss some of the diseases that create the need for vaccination in the first place. Following are the major canine infectious diseases and a simple explanation of each.

Rabies: A devastating viral disease that can be fatal in dogs and people. In fact, vaccination of dogs and cats is an important public-health measure to create a resistant animal buffer population to protect people from contracting the disease. Vaccination schedules are determined on a government level and are not optional for pet owners; rabies vaccination is required by law in all 50 states.

Parvovirus: A severe, potentially life-threatening disease that is easily transmitted between dogs. There are four strains of the virus, but it is believed that there is significant "cross-protection" between strains that may be included in individual vaccines.

Distemper: A potentially severe and life-threatening disease with a relatively high risk of exposure, especially in certain regions. In very high-risk distemper environments, young pups may be vaccinated with human measles vaccine, a related virus that offers cross-protection when administered at four to ten weeks of age.

Hepatitis: Caused by canine adenovirus type 1 (CAV-1), but since vaccination with the causative virus has a higher rate of adverse effects, cross-protection is derived from the use of adenovirus type 2 (CAV-2), a cause of respiratory disease and one of the potential causes of canine cough. Vaccination with CAV-2 provides long-term immunity against hepatitis, but relatively less protection against respiratory infection.

Canine cough: Also called tracheobronchitis, actually a fairly complicated result of viral and bacterial offenders; therefore, even with vaccination, protection is incomplete. Wherever dogs congregate, canine cough will likely be spread among them. Intranasal vaccination with *Bordetella* and parainfluenza is the best safeguard, but the duration of immunity does not appear to be very long, typically a year at most. These are non-core vaccines, but vaccination is sometimes mandated by boarding kennels, obedience classes, dog shows and other places where dogs congregate to try to minimize spread of infection.

Leptospirosis: A potentially fatal disease that is more common in some geographic regions. It is capable of being spread to humans. The disease varies with the individual "serovar," or strain, of *Leptospira* involved. Since there does not appear to be much cross-protection between serovars, protection is only as good as the likelihood that the serovar in the vaccine is the same as the one in the pet's local environment. Problems with *Leptospira* vaccines are that protection does not last very long, side effects are not uncommon and a large percentage of dogs (perhaps 30%) may not respond to vaccination.

Borrelia burgdorferi: The cause of Lyme disease, the risk of which varies with the geographic area in which the pet lives and travels. Lyme disease is spread by deer ticks in the eastern US and western black-legged ticks in the western part of the country, and the risk of exposure is high in some regions. Lameness, fever and inappetence are most commonly seen in affected dogs. The extent of protection from the vaccine has not been conclusively demonstrated.

Coronavirus: This disease has a high risk of exposure, especially in areas where dogs congregate, but it typically causes only mild to moderate digestive upset (diarrhea, vomiting, etc.). Vaccines are available, but the duration of protection is believed to be relatively short and the effectiveness of the vaccine in preventing infection is considered low.

There are many other vaccinations available, including those for *Giardia* and canine adenovirus-1. While there may be some specific indications for their use, and local risk factors to be considered, they are not widely recommended for most dogs.

company that is regulated by your state or province. Many insurance policy look-alikes are actually discount clubs that are redeemable only at specific locations and for specific services. An indemnity plan covers your pet at almost all veterinary, specialty and emergency practices and is an excellent way to manage your pet's ongoing healthcare needs.

VACCINATIONS AND INFECTIOUS DISEASES

There has never been an easier time to prevent a variety of infectious diseases in your dog, but the advances we've made in veterinary medicine come with a price—choice. Now while it may seem that choice is a good thing (and it is), it has never been more difficult for the pet owner (or the veterinarian) to make an informed decision about the best way to protect pets through vaccination.

Years ago, it was just accepted that puppies got a starter series of vaccinations and then annual "boosters" throughout their lives to keep them protected. As more and more vaccines became available, consumers wanted the convenience of having all of that protection in a single injection. The result was "multivalent" vaccines that crammed a lot of protection into a single syringe. The manufacturers' recommendations were to give the vaccines

SAMPLE VACCINATION SCHEDULE

6–8 weeks of age	Parvovirus, Distemper, Adenovirus-2 (Hepatitis)
9–11 weeks of age	Parvovirus, Distemper, Adenovirus-2 (Hepatitis)
12–14 weeks of age	Parvovirus, Distemper, Adenovirus-2 (Hepatitis)
16–20 weeks of age	Rabies
1 year of age	Parvovirus, Distemper, Adenovirus-2 (Hepatitis), Rabies

Revaccination is performed every one to three years, depending on the product, the method of administration and the patient's risk. Initial adult inoculation (for dogs at least 16 weeks of age in which a puppy series was not done or could not be confirmed) is two vaccinations, done three to four weeks apart, with revaccination according to the same criteria mentioned. Other vaccines are given as decided between owner and veterinarian.

DON'T EAT THE DAISIES!

Many plants and flowers are beautiful to look at but can be highly toxic if ingested by your dog. Reactions range from abdominal pain and vomiting to convulsions and death. If the following plants are in your home, remove them. If they are outside your house or in your garden, avoid accidents by making sure your dog is never left unsupervised in those locations.

Azalea	Dumb cane	Mescal bean
Belladonna	Dutchman's breeches	Mushrooms
Bird of paradise	Elephant's ear	Nightshade
Bulbs	Hydrangea	Philodendron
Calla lily	Jack-in-the-pulpit	Poinsettia
Cardinal flower	Jasmine	*Prunus* species
Castor bean	Jimsonweed	Tobacco
Chinaberry tree	Larkspur	Yellow jasmine
Daphne	Laurel	Yews, *Taxus* species
	Lily of the valley	

annually, and this was a simple enough protocol to follow. However, as veterinary medicine has become more sophisticated and we have started looking more at healthcare quandaries rather than convenience, it became necessary to reevaluate the situation and deal with some tough questions. It is important to realize that whether or not to use a particular vaccine depends on the risk of contracting the disease against which it protects, the severity of the disease if it is contracted, the duration of immunity provided by the vaccine, the safety of the product and the needs of the individual

animal. In a very general sense, rabies, distemper, hepatitis and parvovirus are considered core vaccine needs, while parainfluenza, *Bordetella bronchiseptica*, leptospirosis, coronavirus and borreliosis (Lyme disease) are considered non-core needs and best reserved for animals that demonstrate reasonable risk of contracting the diseases.

THE GREAT VACCINATION DEBATE
What kinds of questions need to be addressed? When the vet injects multiple organisms at the same time, might some of the components interfere with one

another in the development of immunologic protection? We don't have the comprehensive answer for that question, but it does appear that the immune system better handles agents when given individually. Unfortunately, most manufacturers still bundle their vaccine components because that is what most pet owners want, so getting vaccines with single components can sometimes be difficult.

Another question has to do with how often vaccines should be given. Again, this seems to be different for each vaccine component. There seems to be a general consensus that a puppy (or a dog with an unknown vaccination history) should get a series of vaccinations to initially stimulate his immunity and then a booster at one year of age, but even the veterinary associations and colleges have trouble reaching agreement about what he should get after that. Rabies vaccination schedules are not debated, because vaccine schedules for this contagious and devastating disease are determined by government agencies. Regarding the rest, some recommend that we continue to give the vaccines annually because this method has worked well as a disease preventive for decades and delivers predictable protection. Others recommend that some of the

vaccines need to be given only every second or third year, as this can be done without affecting levels of protection. This is probably true for some vaccine components (such as hepatitis), but there have been no large studies to demonstrate what the optimal interval should be and whether the same principles hold true for all breeds.

It may be best to just measure titers, which are protective blood levels of various vaccine components, on an annual basis, but that too is not without controversy. Scientists have not precisely determined the minimum titer of specific vaccine components that will be guaranteed to provide a pet with protection. Pets with very high titers will clearly be protected and those with very low titers will need repeat vaccinations, but there is also a large "gray zone" of pets that probably have intermediate protection and may or may not need repeat vaccination, depending on their risk of coming into contact with the disease.

These questions leave primary-care veterinarians in a very uncomfortable position, one that is not easy to resolve. Do they recommend annual vaccination in a manner that has demonstrated successful protection for decades, do they recommend skipping vaccines some years and hope that the protection lasts or do they

The Basenji's upright ears have the advantage of good air circulation but also run the risk of dirt, debris or foreign matter getting inside. Check and clean the ears regularly.

measure blood tests (titers) and hope that the results are convincing enough to clearly indicate whether repeat vaccination is warranted?

These aren't the only vaccination questions impacting pets, owners and veterinarians. Other controversies focus on whether vaccines should be dosed according to body weight (currently they are administered in uniform doses, regardless of the animal's size), whether there are breed-specific issues important in determining vaccination programs (for instance, we know that some breeds have a harder time mounting an appropriate immune response to parvovirus vaccine and might benefit from a different dose or injection interval) and which type of vaccine—live-virus or inactivated—offers more advantages with fewer disadvantages. Clearly, there are many more questions than there are answers. The important thing, as a pet owner, is to be aware of the issues and be able to work with your veterinarian to make decisions that are right for your pet. Be informed and you will appreciate the deliberation required in tailoring a vaccination program to best meet the needs of your pet. Expect also that this is an ongoing, ever-changing topic of debate; thus, the decisions you make this year won't necessarily be the same as the ones you make next year.

NEUTERING/SPAYING

Sterilization procedures (neutering for males/spaying for females) are meant to accomplish several purposes. While the underlying premise is to address the risk of pet overpopulation, there are also some medical and behavioral benefits to the surgeries as well. For females, spaying prior to the first estrus (heat cycle) leads to a marked reduction in the risk of mammary cancer. There also will be no manifestations of "heat" to attract male dogs and no bleeding in the house. For males, there is prevention of testicular cancer and a

PROBLEM: AND THAT STARTS WITH "P"

Urinary tract problems more commonly affect female dogs, especially those who have been spayed. The first sign that a urinary tract problem exists usually is a strong odor from the urine or an unusual color. Blood in the urine, known as hematuria, is another sign of an infection, related to cystitis, a bladder infection, bladder cancer or a blood-clotting disorder. Urinary tract problems can also be signaled by the dog's straining while urinating, experiencing pain during urination and genital discharge as well as excessive water intake and urination.

Excessive drinking, in and of itself, does not indicate a urinary tract problem. A dog who is drinking more than normal may have a kidney or liver problem, a hormonal disorder or diabetes mellitus, or, in the Basenji, Fanconi syndrome. Behaviorists report a disorder known as psychogenic polydipsia, which manifests itself in excessive drinking and urination. If you notice your dog drinking much more than normal, take him to the vet.

do indeed prevent animals from contributing to pet overpopulation, even no-cost and low-cost neutering options have not eliminated the problem. Perhaps one of the main reasons for this is that individuals who intentionally breed their dogs and those who allow their animals to run at large are the main causes of unwanted offspring. Also, animals in shelters are often there because they were abandoned or relinquished, not because they came from unplanned matings. Neutering/spaying is important, but it should be considered in the context of the real causes of animals' ending up in shelters and eventually being euthanized.

One of the important considerations regarding neutering is

reduction in the risk of prostate problems. In both sexes, there may be some limited reduction in aggressive behaviors toward other dogs, and some diminishing of urine marking, roaming and mounting.

While neutering and spaying

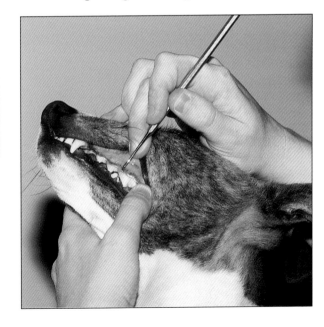

A thorough dental scraping will be done by the vet; only experienced owners should attempt this at home, as it could cause injury if done incorrectly.

Proper eye care is a necessity for all dogs. See the vet if any eye problems occur and follow his instructions as to how to administer properly any prescribed medication.

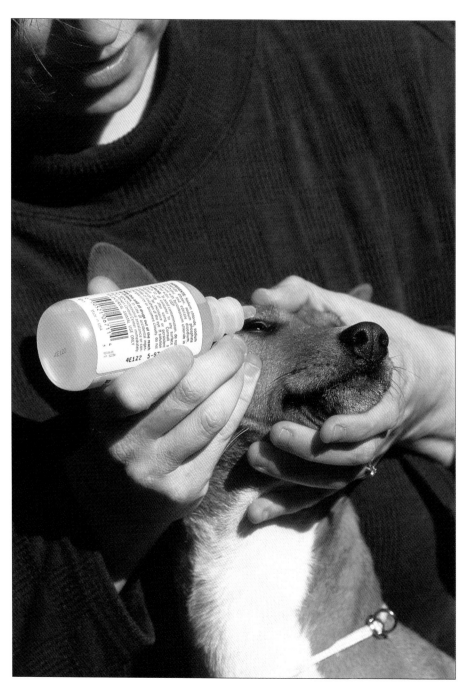

that it is a surgical procedure. This sometimes gets lost in discussions of low-cost procedures and commoditization of the process. In females, spaying is specifically referred to as an ovariohysterectomy. In this procedure, a midline incision is made in the abdomen and the entire uterus and both ovaries are surgically removed. While this is a major invasive surgical procedure, it usually has few complications, because it is typically performed on healthy young animals. However, it is major surgery, as any woman who has had a hysterectomy will attest.

In males, neutering has traditionally referred to castration, which involves the surgical removal of both testicles. While still a significant piece of surgery, there is not the abdominal exposure that is required in the female surgery. In addition, there is now a chemical sterilization option, in which a solution is injected into each testicle, leading to atrophy of the sperm-producing cells. This can typically be done under sedation rather than full anesthesia. This is a relatively new approach, and there are no long-term clinical studies yet available.

Neutering/spaying is typically done around six months of age at most veterinary hospitals, although techniques have been

Be aware of dangers that lurk outdoors—fertilizers, poisonous plants, insects, parasites and the like.

pioneered to perform the procedures in animals as young as eight weeks of age. In general, the surgeries on the very young animals are done for the specific reason of sterilizing them before they go to their new homes. This is done in some shelter hospitals for assurance that the animals will definitely not produce any pups. Otherwise, these organizations need to rely on owners to comply with their wishes to have the animals "altered" at a later date, something that does not always happen.

There are some exciting immunocontraceptive "vaccines" currently under development, and there may be a time when contraception in pets will not require surgical procedures. We anxiously await these developments.

EXTERNAL PARASITES

FLEAS

Fleas have been around for millions of years and, while we have better tools now for controlling them than at any time in the past, there still is little chance that they will end up on an endangered species list. Actually, they are very well adapted to living on our pets, and they continue to adapt as we make advances.

The female flea can consume 15 times her weight in blood during active reproduction and can lay as many as 40 eggs a day. These eggs are very resistant to the effects of insecticides. They hatch into larvae, which then mature and spin cocoons. The immature fleas reside in this pupal stage until the time is right for feeding. This pupal stage is also very resistant to the effects of insecticides, and pupae can last in the environment without feeding for many months. Newly emergent fleas are attracted to animals by the warmth of the animals' bodies, movement and exhaled carbon dioxide. However, when they first emerge from their cocoons, they orient towards light; thus when an animal passes between a flea and the light source, casting a shadow, the flea pounces and starts to feed. If the animal turns out to be a dog or cat, the reproductive cycle continues. If the flea lands on another type of animal, including a person, the flea will bite but will then look for a more appropriate host. An emerging adult flea can survive without feeding for up to 12 months but, once it tastes blood, it can survive off its host for only three to four days.

It was once thought that fleas spend most of their lives in the environment, but we now know that fleas won't willingly jump off a dog unless leaping to another dog or when physically removed by brushing, bathing or other manipulation. Flea eggs, on the other hand, are shiny and smooth, and they roll off the animal and into the environment. The eggs, larvae and pupae then exist in the environment, but once the adult finds a susceptible animal, it's home sweet home until the flea is forced to seek refuge elsewhere.

Since adult fleas live on the animal and immature forms survive in the environment, a successful treatment plan must address all stages of the flea life cycle. There are now several safe and effective flea-control products that can be applied on a monthly

---

FLEA PREVENTION FOR YOUR DOG

- Discuss with your veterinarian the safest product to protect your dog, likely in the form of a monthly tablet or a liquid preparation placed on the back of the dog's neck.
- For dogs suffering from flea-bite dermatitis, a shampoo or topical insecticide treatment is required.
- Your lawn and property should be sprayed with an insecticide designed to kill fleas and ticks that lurk outdoors.
- Using a flea comb, check the dog's coat regularly for any signs of parasites.
- Practice good housekeeping. Vacuum floors, carpets and furniture regularly, especially in the areas that the dog frequents, and wash the dog's bedding weekly.
- Follow up house-cleaning with carpet shampoos and sprays to rid the house of fleas at all stages of development. Insect growth regulators are the safest option.

---

basis. These include fipronil, imidacloprid, selamectin and permethrin (found in several formulations). Most of these products have significant flea-killing rates within 24 hours. However, none of them will control the immature forms in the environment. To accomplish this, there are a variety of insect growth regulators that can be

THE FLEA'S LIFE CYCLE

What came first, the flea or the egg? This age-old mystery is more difficult to comprehend than the actual cycle of the flea. Fleas usually live only about four months. A female can lay 2,000 eggs in her lifetime.

Egg

After ten days of rolling around your carpet or under your furniture, the eggs hatch into larvae, which feed on various and sundry debris. In days or months, depending on the climate, the larvae spin cocoons and develop into the pupal or nymph stage, which quickly develop into fleas.

Larva

Pupa

These immature fleas must locate a host within 10 to 14 days or they will die. Only about 1% of the flea population exist as adult fleas, while the other 99% exist as eggs, larvae or pupae.

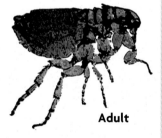

Adult

KILL FLEAS THE NATURAL WAY

If you choose not to go the route of conventional medication, there are some natural ways to ward off fleas:

• Dust your dog with a natural flea powder, composed of such herbal goodies as rosemary, wormwood, pennyroyal, citronella, rue, tobacco powder and eucalyptus.

• Apply diatomaceous earth, the fossilized remains of single-cell algae, to your carpets, furniture and pet's bedding. Even though it's not good for dogs, it's even worse for fleas, which will dry up swiftly and die.

• Brush your dog frequently, give him adequate exercise and let him fast occasionally. All of these activities strengthen the dog's system and make him more resistant to disease and parasites.

• Bathe your dog with a capful of pennyroyal or eucalyptus oil.

• Feed a natural diet, free of additives and preservatives. Add some fresh garlic and brewer's yeast to the dog's morning portion, as these items have flea-repelling properties.

sprayed into the environment (e.g., pyriproxyfen, methoprene, fenoxycarb) as well as insect development inhibitors such as lufenuron that can be administered. These compounds have no effect on adult fleas, but they stop immature forms from developing into adults. In years gone by we relied heavily on toxic insecticides (such as organophosphates, organochlorines and carbamates) to manage the flea problem, but today's options are not only much safer to use on our pets but also safer for the environment.

TICKS

Ticks are members of the spider class (arachnids) and are blood-sucking parasites capable of transmitting a variety of diseases, including Lyme disease, ehrlichiosis, babesiosis and Rocky Mountain spotted fever. It's easy to see ticks on your own skin, but it is more of a challenge when your furry companion is affected. Whenever you happen to be planning a stroll in a tick-infested area (especially forests, grassy or wooded areas or parks) be prepared to do a thorough inspection of your dog afterward to search for ticks. Ticks can be tricky, so make sure you spend time looking in the ears, between the toes and everywhere else where a tick might hide. Ticks need to be attached for 24–72 hours before they transmit most of the diseases that they carry, so you do have a window of opportunity for some preventive intervention.

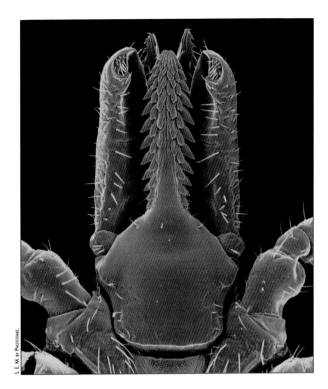

S. E. M. BY PHOTOTAKE.

A scanning electron micrograph of the head of a female deer tick, *Ixodes dammini*, a parasitic tick that carries Lyme disease.

A TICKING BOMB

There is nothing good about a tick's harpooning his nose into your dog's skin. Among the diseases caused by ticks are Rocky Mountain spotted fever, canine ehrlichiosis, canine babesiosis, canine hepatozoonosis and Lyme disease. If a dog is allergic to the saliva of a female wood tick, he can develop tick paralysis.

Female ticks live to eat and breed. They can lay between 4,000 and 5,000 eggs and they die soon after. Males, on the other hand, live only to mate with the females and continue the process as long as they are able. Most ticks live on multiple hosts before parasitizing dogs. The immature forms typically reside on grass and shrubs, waiting for susceptible animals to walk by. The larvae and nymph stages typically feed on wildlife.

If only a few ticks are present on a dog, they can be plucked out, but it is important to remove the entire head and mouthparts,

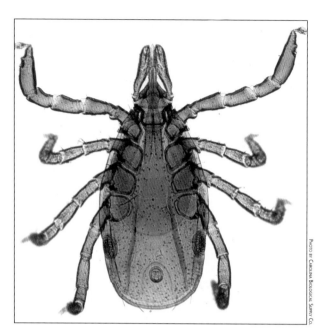

Deer tick,
Ixodes dammini.

which may be deeply embedded in the skin. This is best accomplished with forceps designed especially for this purpose; fingers can be used but should be protected with rubber gloves, plastic wrap or at least a paper towel. The tick should be grasped as closely as possible to the animal's skin and should be pulled upward with steady, even pressure. Do not squeeze, crush or puncture the body of the tick or you risk exposure to any disease carried by that tick. Once the ticks have been removed, the sites of attachment should be disinfected. Your hands should then be washed with soap and water to further minimize risk of contagion. The tick should be

disposed of in a container of alcohol or household bleach.

Some of the newer flea products, specifically those with fipronil, selamectin and permethrin, have effect against some, but not all, species of tick. Flea collars containing appropriate pesticides (e.g., propoxur, chlorfenvinphos) can aid in tick control. In most areas, such collars should be placed on animals in March, at the beginning of the tick season, and changed regularly. Leaving the collar on when the pesticide level is waning invites the development of resistance. Amitraz collars are also good for tick control, and the active ingredient does not interfere with other flea-control products. The ingredient helps prevent the attachment of ticks to the skin and will cause those ticks already on the skin to detach themselves.

TICK CONTROL

Removal of underbrush and leaf litter and the thinning of trees in areas where tick control is desired are recommended. These actions remove the cover and food sources for small animals that serve as hosts for ticks. With continued mowing of grasses in these areas, the probability of ticks' surviving is further reduced. A variety of insecticide ingredients (e.g., resmethrin, carbaryl, permethrin, chlorpyrifos, dioxathion and allethrin) are registered for tick control around the home.

MITES

Mites are tiny arachnid parasites that parasitize the skin of dogs. Skin diseases caused by mites are referred to as "mange," and there are many different forms seen in dogs. These forms are very different from one another, each one warranting an individual description.

Sarcoptic mange, or scabies, is one of the itchiest conditions that affects dogs. The microscopic *Sarcoptes* mites burrow into the superficial layers of the skin and can drive dogs crazy with itchiness. They are also communicable to people, although they can't complete their reproductive cycle on people. In addition to being tiny, the mites also are often difficult to find when trying to make a diagnosis. Skin scrapings from multiple areas are examined microscopically but, even then, sometimes the mites cannot be found.

Fortunately, scabies is relatively easy to treat, and there are a variety of products that will successfully kill the mites. Since the mites can't live in the environment for very long without feeding, a complete cure is usually possible within four to eight weeks.

Cheyletiellosis is caused by a relatively large mite, which sometimes can be seen even without a microscope. Often referred to as "walking dandruff," this also causes itching, but not usually as profound as with scabies.

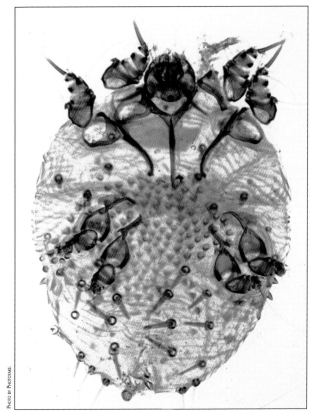

PHOTO BY PHOTOTAKE.

Sarcoptes scabiei, commonly known as the "itch mite."

While *Cheyletiella* mites can survive somewhat longer in the environment than scabies mites, they too are relatively easy to treat, being responsive to not only the medications used to treat scabies but also often to flea-control products.

Otodectes cynotis is the canine ear mite and is one of the more common causes of mange, especially in young dogs in shelters or pet stores. That's because the mites are typically present in large numbers and are quickly spread to

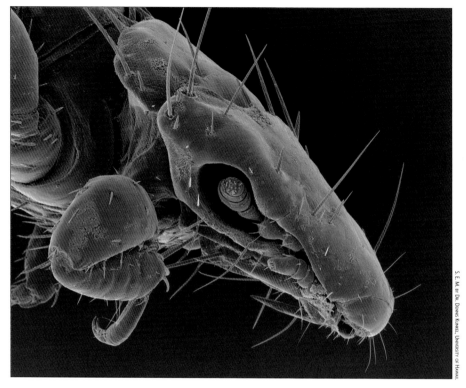

Micrograph of a dog louse, *Heterodoxus spiniger*. Female lice attach their eggs to the hairs of the dog. As the eggs hatch, the larval lice bite and feed on the blood. Lice can also feed on dead skin and hair. This feeding activity can cause hair loss and skin problems.

S. E. M. BY DR. DENNIS KUNKEL, UNIVERSITY OF HAWAII

nearby animals. The mites rarely do much harm but can be difficult to eradicate if the treatment regimen is not comprehensive. While many try to treat the condition with ear drops only, this is the most common cause of treatment failure. Ear drops cause the mites to simply move out of the ears and as far away as possible (usually to the base of the tail) until the insecticide levels in the ears drop to an acceptable level—then it's back to business as usual! The successful treatment of ear mites requires treating all animals in the household with a systemic insecticide, such as selamectin, or a combination of miticidal ear drops combined with whole-body flea-control preparations.

Demodicosis, sometimes referred to as red mange, can be one of the most difficult forms of mange to treat. Part of the problem has to do with the fact that the mites live in the hair follicles and they are relatively well shielded from topical and systemic products. The main issue, however, is that demodectic mange typically results only when there is some underlying process interfering with the dog's immune system.

Since *Demodex* mites are

normal residents of the skin of mammals, including humans, there is usually a mite population explosion only when the immune system fails to keep the number of mites in check. In young animals, the immune deficit may be transient or may reflect an actual inherited immune problem. In older animals, demodicosis is usually seen only when there is another disease hampering the immune system, such as diabetes, cancer, thyroid problems or the use of immune-suppressing drugs. Accordingly, treatment involves not only trying to kill the mange mites but also discerning what is interfering with immune function and correcting it if possible.

Chiggers represent several different species of mite that don't parasitize dogs specifically, but do latch on to passersby and can cause irritation. The problem is most prevalent in wooded areas in the late summer and fall. Treatment is not difficult, as the mites do not complete their life cycle on dogs and are susceptible to a variety of miticidal products.

Mosquitoes

Mosquitoes have long been known to transmit a variety of diseases to people, as well as just being biting pests during warm weather. They also pose a real risk to pets. Not only do they carry deadly heartworms but recently there also has been much concern over their involvement with West Nile virus. While we can avoid heartworm with the use of preventive medications, there are no such preventives for West Nile virus. The only method of prevention in endemic areas is active mosquito control. Fortunately, most dogs that have been exposed to the virus only developed flu-like symptoms and, to date, there have not been the large number of reported deaths in canines as seen in some other species.

Illustration of *Demodex folliculoram*.

ILLUSTRATION BY PHOTOTAKE

MOSQUITO REPELLENT

Low concentrations of DEET (less than 10%), found in many human mosquito repellents, have been safely used in dogs but, in these concentrations, probably give only about two hours of protection. DEET may be safe in these small concentrations, but since it is not licensed for use on dogs, there is no research proving its safety for dogs. Products containing permethrin give the longest-lasting protection, perhaps two to four weeks. As DEET is not licensed for use on dogs, and both DEET and permethrin can be quite toxic to cats, appropriate care should be exercised. Other products, such as those containing oil of citronella, also have some mosquito-repellent activity, but typically have a relatively short duration of action.

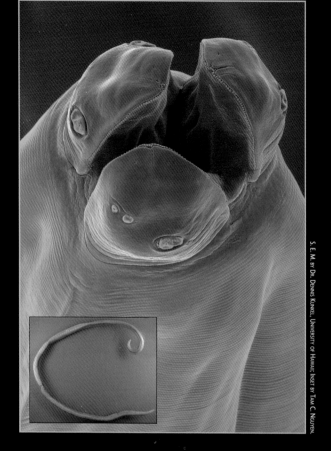

S. E. M. BY DR. DENNIS KUNKEL, UNIVERSITY OF HAWAII. INSET BY TAM C. NGUYEN.

ASCARID DANGERS

The most commonly encountered worms in dogs are roundworms known as ascarids. *Toxascaris leonine* and *Toxocara canis* are the two species that infect dogs. Subsisting in the dog's stomach and intestines, adult roundworms can grow to 7 inches in length and adult females can lay in excess of 200,000 eggs in a single day.

In humans, visceral larval migrans affects people who have ingested eggs of *Toxocara canis*, which frequently contaminates children's sandboxes, beaches and park grounds. The roundworms reside in the human's stomach and intestines, as they would in a dog's, but do not mature. Instead, they find their way to the liver, lungs and skin, or even to the heart or kidneys in severe cases. Deworming puppies is critical in preventing the infection in humans, and young children should never handle nursing pups who have not been dewormed.

The ascarid roundworm *Toxocara canis*, showing the mouth with three lips. INSET: Photomicrograph of the roundworm *Ascaris lumbricoides.*

INTERNAL PARASITES: WORMS

ASCARIDS

Ascarids are intestinal roundworms that rarely cause severe disease in dogs. Nonetheless, they are of major public health significance because they can be transferred to people. Sadly, it is children who are most commonly affected by the parasite, probably from inadvertently ingesting ascarid-contaminated soil. In fact, many yards and children's sandboxes contain appreciable numbers of ascarid eggs. So, while ascarids don't bite dogs or latch onto their intestines to suck blood, they do cause some nasty medical conditions in children and are best eradicated from our furry friends. Because pups can start passing ascarid eggs by three weeks of age, most parasite-control programs begin at two weeks of age and are repeated every two weeks until pups are eight weeks old. It is important to

S. E. M. BY DR. DENNIS KUNKEL, UNIVERSITY OF HAWAII.

realize that bitches can pass ascarids to their pups even if they test negative prior to whelping. Accordingly, bitches are best treated at the same time as the pups.

HOOKWORMS

Unlike ascarids, hookworms do latch onto a dog's intestinal tract and can cause significant loss of blood and protein. Similar to ascarids, hookworms can be transmitted to humans, where they cause a condition known as cutaneous larval migrans. Dogs can become infected either by consuming the infective larvae or by the larvae's penetrating the skin directly. People most often get infected when they are lying on the ground (such as on a beach) and the larvae penetrate the skin. Yes, the larvae can penetrate through a beach blanket. Hookworms are typically susceptible to the same medications used to treat ascarids.

The hookworm *Ancylostoma caninum* infests the intestines of dogs. INSET: Note the row of hooks at the posterior end, used to anchor the worm to the intestinal wall.

WHIPWORMS

Whipworms latch onto the lower aspects of the dog's colon and can cause cramping and diarrhea. Eggs do not start to appear in the dog's feces until about three months after the dog was infected. This worm has a peculiar life cycle, which makes it more difficult to control than ascarids or hookworms. The good thing is that whipworms rarely are transferred to people.

Some of the medications used to treat ascarids and hookworms are also effective against whipworms, but, in general, a separate treatment protocol is needed. Since most of the medications are effective against the adults but not the eggs or larvae, treatment is typically repeated in three weeks, and then often in three

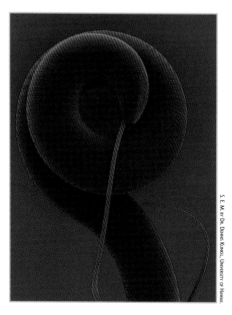

Adult whipworm, *Trichuris* sp., an intestinal parasite.

S. E. M. BY DR. DENNIS KUNKEL, UNIVERSITY OF HAWAII.

> ## WORM-CONTROL GUIDELINES
> • Practice sanitary habits with your dog and home.
> • Clean up after your dog and don't let him sniff or eat other dogs' droppings.
> • Control insects and fleas in the dog's environment. Fleas, lice, cockroaches, beetles, mice and rats can act as hosts for various worms.
> • Prevent dogs from eating uncooked meat, raw poultry and dead animals.
> • Keep dogs and children from playing in sand and soil.
> • Kennel dogs on cement or gravel; avoid dirt runs.
> • Administer heartworm preventives regularly.
> • Have your vet examine your dog's stools at your annual visits.
> • Select a boarding kennel carefully so as to avoid contamination from other dogs or an unsanitary environment.
> • Prevent dogs from roaming. Obey local leash laws.

months as well. Unfortunately, since dogs don't develop resistance to whipworms, it is difficult to prevent them from getting reinfected if they visit soil contaminated with whipworm eggs.

TAPEWORMS

There are many different species of tapeworm that affect dogs, but *Dipylidium caninum* is probably the most common and is spread by fleas. Flea larvae feed on organic debris and tapeworm eggs in the environment and, when a dog chews at himself and manages to ingest fleas, he might get a dose of tapeworm at the same time. The tapeworm then develops further in the intestine of the dog.

The tapeworm itself, which is a parasitic flatworm that latches onto the intestinal wall, is composed of numerous segments. When the segments break off into the intestine (as proglottids), they may accumulate around the rectum, like grains of rice. While this tapeworm is disgusting in its behavior, it is not directly communicable to humans (although humans can also get infected by swallowing fleas).

A much more dangerous flatworm is *Echinococcus multilocularis*, which is typically found in foxes, coyotes and wolves. The eggs are passed in the feces and infect rodents, and, when dogs eat the rodents, the dogs can be infected by thousands of adult tapeworms. While the parasites don't cause many problems in dogs, this is considered the most lethal worm infection that people can get. Take appropriate precautions if you live in an area in which these tapeworms are found. Do not use mulch that may contain feces of dogs, cats or wildlife, and discourage your pets from hunting wildlife. Treat these tapeworm infections aggressively in pets, because if humans get infected, approximately half die.

HEARTWORMS

Heartworm disease is caused by the parasite *Dirofilaria immitis* and is seen in dogs around the world. A member of the roundworm group, it is spread between dogs by the bite of an infected mosquito. The mosquito injects infective larvae into the dog's skin with its bite, and these larvae develop under the skin for a period of time before making their way to the heart. There they develop into adults, which grow and create blockages of the heart, lungs and major blood vessels there. They also start producing offspring (microfilariae) and these microfilariae circulate in

A dog tapeworm proglottid (body segment).

The dog tapeworm *Taenia pisiformis.*

A Look at Internal Parasites

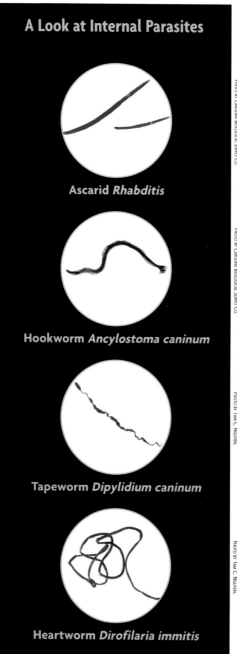

Ascarid *Rhabditis*

Hookworm *Ancylostoma caninum*

Tapeworm *Dipylidium caninum*

Heartworm *Dirofilaria immitis*

Photo by Carolina Biological Supply Co.

Photo by Carolina Biological Supply Co.

Photo by Tam C. Nguyen.

Photo by Tam C. Nguyen.

the bloodstream, waiting to hitch a ride when the next mosquito bites. Once in the mosquito, the microfilariae develop into infective larvae and the entire process is repeated.

When dogs get infected with heartworm, over time they tend to develop symptoms associated with heart disease, such as coughing, exercise intolerance and potentially many other manifestations. Diagnosis is confirmed by either seeing the microfilariae themselves in blood samples or using immunologic tests (antigen testing) to identify the presence of adult heartworms. Since antigen tests measure the presence of adult heartworms and microfilarial tests measure offspring produced by adults, neither are positive until six to seven months after the initial infection. However, the beginning of damage can occur by fifth-stage larvae as early as three months after infection. Thus it is possible for dogs to be harboring problem-causing larvae for up to three months before either type of test would identify an infection.

The good news is that there are great protocols available for preventing heartworm in dogs. Testing is critical in the process, and it is important to understand the benefits as well as the limitations of such testing. All dogs six months of age or older that have not been on continuous heart-

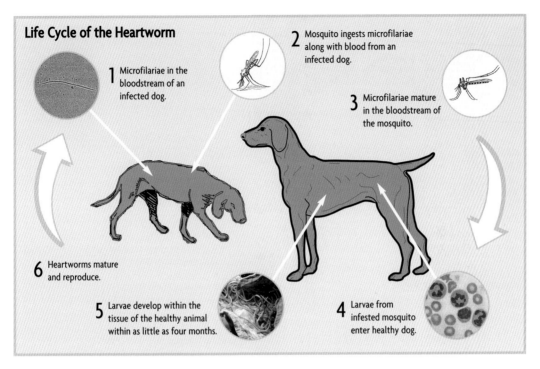

Life Cycle of the Heartworm

1 Microfilariae in the bloodstream of an infected dog.

2 Mosquito ingests microfilariae along with blood from an infected dog.

3 Microfilariae mature in the bloodstream of the mosquito.

4 Larvae from infested mosquito enter healthy dog.

5 Larvae develop within the tissue of the healthy animal within as little as four months.

6 Heartworms mature and reproduce.

worm-preventive medication should be screened with microfilarial or antigen tests. For dogs receiving preventive medication, periodic antigen testing helps assess the effectiveness of the preventives. The American Heartworm Society guidelines suggest that annual retesting may not be necessary when owners have absolutely provided continuous heartworm prevention. Retesting on a two- to three-year interval may be sufficient in these cases. However, your veterinarian will likely have specific guidelines under which heartworm preventives will be prescribed, and many prefer to err on the side of safety and retest annually.

It is indeed fortunate that heartworm is relatively easy to prevent, because treatments can be as life-threatening as the disease itself. Treatment requires a two-step process that kills the adult heartworms first and then the microfilariae. Prevention is obviously preferable; this involves a once-monthly oral or topical treatment. The most common oral preventives include ivermectin (not suitable for some breeds), moxidectin and milbemycin oxime; the once-a-month topical drug selamectin provides heartworm protection in addition to flea, tick and other parasite controls.

THE **ABC**s OF
Emergency Care

Abrasions
Clean wound with running water or 3% hydrogen peroxide. Pat dry with gauze and spray with antibiotic. Do not cover.

Animal Bites
Clean area with soap and saline solution or water. Apply pressure to any bleeding area. Apply antibiotic ointment.

Antifreeze Poisoning
Induce vomiting and take dog to the vet.

Bee Sting
Remove stinger and apply soothing lotion or cold compress; give antihistamine in proper dosage.

Bleeding
Apply pressure directly to wound with gauze or towel for five to ten minutes. If wound does not stop bleeding, wrap wound with gauze and adhesive tape.

Bloat/Gastric Torsion
Immediately take the dog to the vet or emergency clinic; phone from car. No time to waste.

Burns
Chemical: Bathe dog with water and pet shampoo. Rinse in saline solution. Apply antibiotic ointment.

Acid: Rinse with water. Apply one part baking soda, two parts water to affected area.

Alkali: Rinse with water. Apply one part vinegar, four parts water to affected area.

Electrical: Apply antibiotic ointment. Seek veterinary assistance immediately.

Choking
If the dog is on the verge of collapsing, wedge a solid object, such as the handle of screwdriver, between molars on one side of the mouth to keep mouth open. Pull tongue out. Use long-nosed pliers or fingers to remove foreign object. Do not push the object down the dog's throat. For small or medium dogs, hold dog upside down by hind legs and shake firmly to dislodge foreign object.

Chlorine Ingestion
With clean water, rinse the mouth and eyes. Give the dog water to drink; contact the vet.

Constipation
Feed dog 2 tablespoons bran flakes with each meal. Encourage drinking water. Mix 1/4 teaspoon mineral oil in dog's food.

Diarrhea
Withhold food for 12 to 24 hours. Feed dog antidiarrheal with eyedropper. When feeding resumes, feed one part boiled hamburger, one part plain cooked rice, 1/4 to 3/4 cup four times daily.

Dog Bite
Snip away hair around puncture wound; clean with 3% hydrogen peroxide; apply tincture of iodine. If wound appears deep, take the dog to the vet.

Frostbite
Wrap the dog in a heavy blanket. Warm affected area with a warm bath for ten minutes. Red color to skin will return with circulation; if tissues are pale after 20 minutes, contact the vet.

Use a portable, durable container large enough to contain all items

Heat Stroke
Partially submerge the dog in cold water; if no response within ten minutes, contact the vet.

Hot Spots
Mix 2 packets Domeboro® with 2 cups water. Saturate cloth with mixture and apply to hot spots for 15 to 30 minutes. Apply antibiotic ointment. Repeat every six to eight hours.

Poisonous Plants
Wash affected area with soap and water. Cleanse with alcohol. For foxtail/grass, apply antibiotic ointment.

Rat Poison Ingestion
Induce vomiting. Keep dog calm, maintain dog's normal body temperature (use blanket or heating pad). Get to the vet for antidote.

Shock
Keep the dog calm and warm; call for veterinary assistance.

Snake Bite
If possible, bandage the area and apply pressure. If the area is not conducive to bandaging, use ice to control bleeding. Get immediate help from the vet.

Tick Removal
Apply flea and tick spray directly on tick. Wait one minute. Using tweezers or wearing plastic gloves, apply constant pull while grasping tick's body. Apply antibiotic ointment.

Vomiting
Restrict dog's water intake; offer a few ice cubes. Withhold food for next meal. Contact vet if vomiting persists longer than 24 hours.

DOG OWNER'S FIRST-AID KIT
- ❑ Gauze bandages/swabs
- ❑ Adhesive and non-adhesive bandages
- ❑ Antibiotic powder
- ❑ Antiseptic wash
- ❑ Hydrogen peroxide 3%
- ❑ Antibiotic ointment
- ❑ Lubricating jelly
- ❑ Rectal thermometer
- ❑ Nylon muzzle
- ❑ Scissors and forceps
- ❑ Eyedropper
- ❑ Syringe
- ❑ Anti-bacterial/fungal solution
- ❑ Saline solution
- ❑ Antihistamine
- ❑ Cotton balls
- ❑ Nail clippers
- ❑ Screwdriver/pen knife
- ❑ Flashlight
- ❑ Emergency phone numbers

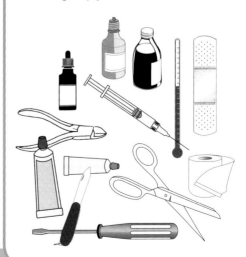

Number-One Killer Disease in Dogs: CANCER

In every age, there is a word associated with a disease or plague that causes humans to shudder. In the 21st century, that word is "cancer." Just as cancer is the leading cause of death in humans, it claims nearly half the lives of dogs that die from a natural disease as well as half the dogs that die over the age of ten years.

Described as a genetic disease, cancer becomes a greater risk as the dog ages. Vets and dog owners have become increasingly aware of the threat of cancer to dogs. Statistics reveal that one dog in every five will develop cancer, the most common of which is skin cancer. Many cancers, including prostate, ovarian and breast cancer, can be avoided by spaying and neutering our dogs by the age of six months.

Early detection of cancer can save or extend a dog's life, so it is absolutely vital for owners to have their dogs examined by a qualified vet or oncologist immediately upon detection of any abnormality. Certain dietary guidelines have also proven to reduce the onset and spread of cancer. Foods based on fish rather than beef, due to the presence of Omega-3 fatty acids, are recommended. Other amino acids such as glutamine have significant benefits for canines, particularly those breeds that show a greater susceptibility to cancer.

Cancer management and treatments promise hope for future generations of canines. Since the disease is genetic, breeders should never breed a dog whose parents, grandparents and any related siblings have developed cancer. It is difficult to know whether to exclude an otherwise healthy dog from a breeding program, as the disease does not manifest itself until the dog's senior years.

RECOGNIZE CANCER WARNING SIGNS

Since early detection can possibly rescue your dog from becoming a cancer statistic, it is essential for owners to recognize the possible signs and seek the assistance of a qualified professional.

- Abnormal bumps or lumps that continue to grow
- Bleeding or discharge from any body cavity
- Persistent stiffness or lameness
- Recurrent sores or sores that do not heal
- Inappetence
- Breathing difficulties
- Weight loss
- Bad breath or odors
- General malaise and fatigue
- Eating and swallowing problems
- Difficulty urinating and defecating

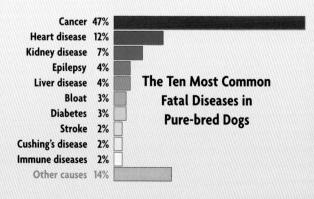

Cancer	47%
Heart disease	12%
Kidney disease	7%
Epilepsy	4%
Liver disease	4%
Bloat	3%
Diabetes	3%
Stroke	2%
Cushing's disease	2%
Immune diseases	2%
Other causes	14%

The Ten Most Common Fatal Diseases in Pure-bred Dogs

Cognitive Dysfunction Syndrome

"Old-Dog Syndrome"

There are many ways for you to evaluate old-dog syndrome. Veterinarians have defined CDS (cognitive dysfunction syndrome) as the gradual deterioration of cognitive abilities, indicated by changes in the dog's behavior. When a dog changes his routine response, and maladies have been eliminated as the cause of these behavioral changes, then CDS is the usual diagnosis.

More than half the dogs over eight years old suffer from some form of CDS. The older the dog, the more chance he has of suffering from CDS. In humans, doctors often dismiss the CDS behavioral changes as part of "winding down."

There are four major signs of CDS: frequent potty accidents inside the home, sleeping much more or much less than normal, acting confused and failing to respond to social stimuli.

Symptoms of CDS

FREQUENT POTTY ACCIDENTS
- Urinates in the house.
- Defecates in the house.
- Doesn't signal that he wants to go out.

FAILURE TO RESPOND TO SOCIAL STIMULI
- Comes to people less frequently, whether called or not.
- Doesn't tolerate petting for more than a short time.
- Doesn't come to the door when you return home.

CONFUSION
- Goes outside and just stands there.
- Appears confused with a faraway look in his eyes.
- Hides more often.
- Doesn't recognize friends.
- Doesn't come when called.
- Walks around listlessly and without a destination.

SLEEP PATTERNS
- Awakens more slowly.
- Sleeps more than normal during the day.
- Sleeps less during the night.

Is dog showing in your blood? Are you excited by the idea of gaiting your handsome Basenji around the ring to the thunderous applause of an enthusiastic audience? Are you certain that your beloved Basenji is flawless? You are not alone! Every loving owner thinks that his dog has no faults, or too few to mention. No matter how many times an owner reads the breed standard, he cannot find any faults in his aristocratic companion dog. If this sounds like you, and if you are considering entering your Basenji in a dog show, here are some basic questions to ask yourself:

- Did you purchase a "show-quality" puppy from the breeder?
- Is your puppy at least six months of age?
- Does the puppy exhibit correct show type for his breed?
- Does your puppy have any disqualifying faults?
- Is your Basenji registered with the American Kennel Club?
- How much time do you have to devote to training, grooming, conditioning and exhibiting your dog?
- Do you understand the rules and regulations of a dog show?
- Do you have time to learn how to show your dog properly?
- Do you have the financial resources to invest in showing your dog?
- Will you show the dog yourself or hire a professional handler?
- Do you have a vehicle that can accommodate your weekend trips to the dog shows?

The sleek, regal Basenji is a striking presence in show pose.

Success in the show ring requires more than a pretty face, a waggy tail and a pocketful of liver. Even though dog shows can be exciting and enjoyable, the sport of conformation makes great demands on the exhibitors and the dogs. Winning exhibitors live for their dogs, devoting time and money to their dogs' presentation, conditioning and training. Very few novices, even those with good dogs, will find themselves in the winners' circle, though it does happen. Don't be disheartened, though. Every exhibitor began as a novice and worked his way up to the Group ring. It's the "working your way up" part that you must keep in mind.

Assuming that you have purchased a puppy of the correct type and quality for showing, let's begin to examine the world of showing and what's required to get started. Although the entry fee into a dog show is nominal, there are lots of other hidden costs involved with "finishing" your Basenji, that is, making him a champion. Things like equipment, travel, training and

AKC GROUPS

For showing purposes, the American Kennel Club divides its recognized breeds into seven groups: Hounds, Sporting Dogs, Working Dogs, Terriers, Toys, Non-Sporting Dogs and Herding Dogs. The Basenji is in the Hound Group.

conditioning all cost money. A more serious campaign will include fees for a professional handler, boarding, cross-country travel and advertising. Top-winning show dogs can represent a very considerable investment—over $100,000 has been spent in campaigning some dogs. (The investment can be less, of course, for owners who don't use professional handlers.)

Many owners, on the other hand, enter their "average" Basenjis in dog shows for the fun and enjoyment of it. Dog showing makes an absorbing hobby, with many rewards for dogs and owners alike. If you're having fun, meeting other people who share your interests and enjoying the overall experience, you likely will catch the "bug." Once the dog-show bug bites, its effects can last a lifetime; it's certainly much better than a deer tick! Soon you will be envisioning yourself in the center ring at the Westminster Kennel

As the judge goes down the line, she should be comparing each dog in the ring to the breed standard, not to the other dogs.

Basenjis, due to
their small size,
are examined by
show judges on
tables. This
handler uses a
treat to keep the
dog in standing
position during
the judge's
assessment.

Breed winners in a given group compete against each other; this is done for all seven groups. Finally, all seven group winners go head to head in the ring for the Best in Show award.

What most spectators don't understand is the basic idea of conformation. A dog show is often referred to as a "conformation" show. This means that the judge should decide how each dog stacks up (conforms) to the breed standard for his given breed: how well does this Basenji conform to the ideal representative detailed in the standard? Ideally, this is what happens. In reality, however, this ideal often gets slighted as the judge compares Basenji #1 to Basenji #2. Again, the ideal is that each

Club Dog Show in New York City, competing for the prestigious Best in Show cup. This magical dog show is televised annually from Madison Square Garden, and the victorious dog becomes a celebrity overnight.

AKC CONFORMATION SHOWING

Visiting a dog show as a spectator is a great place to start. Pick up the show catalog to find out what time your breed is being shown, who is judging the breed and in which ring the classes will be held. To start, Basenjis compete against other Basenjis, and the winner is selected as Best of Breed by the judge. This is the procedure for each breed. At a group show, all of the Best of Breed winners go on to compete for Group One in their respective groups (the Basenji is in the Hound Group). For example, all Best of

EXPRESS YOURSELF

The most intangible of all canine attributes, expression speaks to the character of the breed, attained by the combined features of the head. The shape and balance of the dog's skull, the color and position of the eyes, the size and carriage of the head and the Basenji's trademark wrinkling mingle to produce the correct expression of the breed. A judge may approach a dog and determine instantly whether the dog's face portrays the desired impression for the breed, conveying nobility, intelligence and alertness among other specifics of the breed standard.

dog is judged based on his merits in comparison to his breed standard, not in comparison to the other dogs in the ring. It is easier for judges to compare dogs of the same breed to decide which they think is the better specimen; in the Group and Best in Show ring, however, it is very difficult to compare one breed to another, like apples to oranges. Thus the dog's conformation to the breed standard—not to mention advertising dollars and good handling—is essential to success in conformation shows. The dog described in the standard (the standard for each AKC breed is written and approved by the breed's national parent club and then submitted to the AKC for approval) is the perfect dog of that breed, and breeders keep their eye on the standard when they choose which dogs to breed, hoping to get closer and closer to the ideal with each litter.

Another good first step for the novice is to join a dog club. You will be astonished by the many and different kinds of dog clubs in the country, with about 5,000 clubs holding events every year. Most clubs require that prospective new members present two letters of recommendation from existing members. Perhaps you've made some friends visiting a show held by a particular club and you would like to join that club. Dog clubs may specialize in a single breed,

like a local or regional Basenji club, or in a specific pursuit, such as obedience, tracking or hunting tests. There are all-breed clubs for all dog enthusiasts; they sponsor

ON THE MOVE

The truest test of a dog's proper structure is his gait, the way the dog moves. The American Kennel Club defines gait as "the pattern of footsteps at various rates of speed, each pattern distinguished by a particular rhythm and footfall." That the dog moves smoothly and effortlessly indicates to the judge that the dog's structure is well made. From the four-beat gallop, the fastest of canine gaits, to the high-lifting hackney gait, each breed varies in its correct gait; not every breed is expected to move in the same way. Each breed standard defines the correct gait for its breed and often identifies movement faults, such as toeing in, side-winding, over-reaching or crossing over.

At the Novice level in an obedience trial, each dog is expected to stay with a group of dogs for a period of time as instructed.

special training days, seminars on topics like grooming or handling or lectures on breeding or canine genetics. There are also clubs that specialize in certain types of dogs, like sighthounds, hunting dogs, companion dogs, etc.

A parent club is the national organization, sanctioned by the AKC, which promotes and safeguards its breed in the country. The Basenji Club of America was formed in 1942 and can be contacted on the Internet at www.basenji.org. The parent club holds an annual national specialty show, usually in a different city each year, in which many of the country's top dogs, handlers and breeders gather to compete. At a specialty show, only members of a single breed are invited to participate. There are also group specialties, in which all members of an AKC group are invited. For more information about dog clubs in your area, contact the AKC at www.akc.org on the Internet or write them at their Raleigh, NC address.

OTHER TYPES OF COMPETITION

In addition to conformation shows, the AKC holds a variety of other competitive events. Obedience trials, agility trials and tracking trials are open to all breeds, while hunting tests, field trials, lure coursing, herding tests and trials, earthdog tests and coonhound events are limited to specific breeds or groups of breeds. The Junior Showmanship program is offered to aspiring young handlers and their dogs, and the Canine Good Citizen® program is an all-around good-behavior test open to all dogs, pure-bred and mixed.

OBEDIENCE TRIALS

Mrs. Helen Whitehouse Walker, a Standard Poodle fancier, can be credited with introducing

---

FOR MORE INFORMATION....

For reliable up-to-date information about registration, dog shows and other canine competitions, contact one of the national registries by mail or via the Internet.

American Kennel Club
5580 Centerview Dr., Raleigh, NC 27606-3390
www.akc.org

United Kennel Club
100 E. Kilgore Road, Kalamazoo, MI 49002
www.ukcdogs.com

Canadian Kennel Club
89 Skyway Ave., Suite 100, Etobicoke, Ontario M9W 6R4 Canada
www.ckc.ca

obedience trials to the United States. In the 1930s, she designed a series of exercises based on those of the Associated Sheep, Police, Army Dog Society of Great Britain. These exercises were intended to evaluate the working relationship between dog and owner. Since those early days of the sport in the US, obedience trials have grown more and more popular, and now more than 2,000 trials each year attract over 100,000 dogs and their owners. Any dog registered with the AKC, regardless of neutering or other disqualifications that would preclude entry in conformation competition, can participate in obedience trials.

There are three levels of difficulty in obedience competition. The first (and easiest) level is the Novice, in which dogs can earn the Companion Dog (CD) title. The intermediate level is the Open level, in which the Companion Dog Excellent (CDX) title is awarded. The advanced level is the Utility level, in which dogs compete for the Utility Dog (UD) title. The first Basenji to earn the UD was Ch. Baranfield's Cyclone. Classes at each level are further divided into "A" and "B," with "A" for beginners and "B" for those with more experience. In order to win a title at a given level, a dog must earn three "legs." A "leg" is accomplished when a dog scores 170 or higher (200 is a perfect score). The scoring system gets a

FIVE CLASSES AT SHOWS

At most AKC all-breed shows, there are five regular classes offered: Puppy, Novice, Bred-by-Exhibitor, American-bred and Open. The Puppy Class is usually divided as 6 to 9 months of age and 9 to 12 months of age. When deciding in which class to enter your dog, whether male or female, you must carefully check the show schedule to make sure that you have selected the right class. Depending on the age of the dog, its previous first-place wins and the sex of the dog, you must make the best choice. It is possible to enter a one-year-old dog who has not won sufficient first places in any of the non-Puppy Classes, though the competition is more intense the further you progress from the Puppy Class.

little trickier when you understand that a dog must score more than 50% of the points available for each exercise in order to actually earn the points. Available points for each exercise range between 20 and 40.

Once he's earned the UD title, a dog can go on to win the prestigious title of Utility Dog Excellent (UDX) by winning "legs" in ten shows. Additionally, Utility Dogs who win "legs" in Open B and Utility B earn points toward the lofty title of Obedience Trial Champion (OTCh.). Established in 1977 by the AKC, this title requires a dog to earn 100 points as well as three first places in a combination of Open B and Utility B classes under three different judges. The "brass ring" of obedience competition is the AKC's National Obedience Invitational. In order to qualify for the invitational, a dog must be ranked in either the top 25 all-breeds in obedience or in the top three for his breed in obedience. The title at stake here is that of National Obedience Champion (NOC).

AGILITY TRIALS

Agility trials became sanctioned by the AKC in August 1994, when the first licensed agility trials were held. Since that time, agility certainly has grown in popularity by leaps and bounds, literally! The AKC allows all registered breeds (including Miscellaneous Class breeds) to participate, providing the dog is 12 months of age or older. Agility is designed so that the handler demonstrates how well the dog can work at his side. The handler directs his dog through, over, under and around an obstacle course that includes jumps, tires, the dog walk, weave poles, pipe tunnels, collapsed tunnels and more. While working his way through the course, the dog must keep one eye and ear on the handler and the rest of his body on the course. The handler runs along with the dog, giving verbal and hand signals to guide the dog through the course.

The first organization to promote agility trials in the US was the United States Dog Agility Association, Inc. (USDAA). Established in 1986, the USDAA sparked the formation of many member clubs around the country. To participate in USDAA trials, dogs must be at least 18 months of age. The USDAA and AKC both offer titles to winning dogs, although the exercises and requirements of the two organizations differ. Agility Dog (AD), Advanced Agility Dog (AAD) and Master Agility Dog (MAD) are the titles offered by the USDAA, while the AKC offers Novice Agility (NA), Open Agility (OA), Agility Excellent (AX) and Master Agility Excellent (MX). Beyond these four AKC titles, dogs can win additional titles in "jumper" classes: Jumper with Weave Novice (NAJ), Open

Agility trials began in the UK in 1977 and, shortly thereafter, the rest of the dog world followed. The Basenji's dexterity makes him a natural at navigating the obstacles on an agility course.

(OAJ) and Excellent (MXJ). The ultimate title in AKC agility is MACH, Master Agility Champion. Dogs can continue to add number designations to the MACH title, indicating how many times the dog has met the title's requirements (MACH1, MACH2 and so on).

Agility trials are a great way to keep your dog active, and they will keep you running, too! You should join a local agility club to learn more about the sport. These clubs offer sessions in which you can introduce your dog to the various obstacles as well as training classes to prepare him for competition. In no time, your dog will be climbing A-frames, crossing the dog walk and flying over hurdles, all with you right beside him. Your heart will leap every time your dog jumps through the hoop—and you'll be having just as much (if not more) fun!

TRACKING

Tracking tests are exciting ways to test your Basenji's keen scenting ability on a competitive level. All dogs have a nose, and all breeds are welcome in tracking tests. The first AKC-licensed tracking test took place in 1937 as part of the Utility level at an obedience trial, and thus competitive tracking was officially begun. The first title, Tracking Dog (TD), was offered in 1947, ten years after the first official tracking test. It was not until 1980 that the AKC added the title Tracking Dog Excellent (TDX), which was followed by the title Versatile Surface Tracking (VST) in 1995. Champion Tracker (CT) is awarded to a dog who has earned all three of those titles. The first Basenji to earn a TD was Ch. Il-Se-Ott Golden Majorette, UDT, owned by Rex Tanaka.

LURE COURSING

Owners of Basenjis have the opportunity to participate in lure coursing. Lure-coursing events are exciting and fast-paced, requiring dogs to follow an artificial lure around a course on an open field. Scores are based on the dog's speed, enthusiasm, agility, endurance and ability to follow the lure. At the non-competitive level, lure coursing is designed to gauge a sighthound's instinctive coursing ability. Competitive lure coursing is more demanding, requiring training and conditioning for a dog to develop his coursing instincts and skills to the fullest, thus preserving the intended function of all sighthound breeds.

Lure coursing on a competitive level is certainly wonderful physical and mental exercise for a dog. A dog must be at least one year of age to enter an AKC coursing event, and he must not have any disqualifications according to his breed standard. Check the AKC's rules and regulations for details. To get started, you can consult the AKC's website to help you find a coursing club in your area. A club can introduce you to the sport and help you learn how to train your dog correctly.

Titles awarded in lure coursing are Junior Courser (JC), Senior Courser (SC) and Master Courser (MC); these are suffix titles, affixed to the end of the dog's name. The Field Champion (FC) title is a prefix title, affixed to the beginning of the dog's name. A Dual Champion is a hound that has earned both a Field Champion title as well as a show championship. Ch. Betsy Ross Flags A Flyin became the first DC in 1980. A Triple Champion (TC) title is awarded to a dog that is a Champion, Field Champion and Obedience Trial Champion. The suffix Lure Courser Excellent (LCX) is given to a dog who has earned the FC title plus 45 additional championship points, and number designations are added to the title upon each additional 45 championship points earned (LCX II, III, IV and so on).

Basenjis also can participate in events sponsored by the American Sighthound Field Association (ASFA), an organization devoted to the pursuit of lure coursing. The ASFA was founded in 1972 as a means of keeping open-field coursing dogs fit during the off-season. The Basenji was approved for ASFA events in 1979. A historic win by Bubalak's Divine Bette occurred on September 3, 1979 when she won

Although Basenjis naturally take to lure coursing, much time, training and dedication are required from the dogs' owners.

Best in Field at the first trial. She became the first Basenji Field Champion later that year.

Dogs must be of an accepted sighthound breed in order to be eligible for participation. Each dog must pass a certification run in which he shows that he can run with another dog without interfering. The course is laid out using pulleys and a motor to drive the string around the pulleys. Normally white plastic bags are used as lures, although real fur strips may also be attached. Dogs run in trios, each handled by their own slipper. The dogs are scored on their endurance, follow, speed, agility and enthusiasm. Dogs earn their Field Champion titles by earning two first places, or one first- and two second-place finishes, as well as accumulating 100 points. They can then go on to earn the LCM title, Lure Courser of Merit, by winning four first places and accumulating 300 additional points. The first LCM was Dokhues Enuf Lovins.

Is there any doubt that the Basenji loves the excitement of the chase?

My Basenji

PUT YOUR PUPPY'S FIRST PICTURE HERE

Dog's Name _____

Date _____ Photographer _____